# CELEBRITY EXERCISE

# THE SECRETS OF EXERCISE SUCCE

Also by the author: STRETCH

OM FAMOUS PEOPLE

# CELEBRITY EXERCISE

**Ann Smith**

*Illustrations by Howard Low*

WALKER AND COMPANY · NEW YORK

First published in the United States of America in 1976 by the Walker Pub-lishing Company, Inc.

Published simultaneously in Canada by Fitzhenry & Whiteside, Limited, Toronto.

ISBN: 0-8027-5333-7

Library of Congress Catalog Card Number: 75-12188

Printed in the United States of America.

10  9  8  7  6  5  4  3  2

# CONTENTS

# INTRODUCTION

DURING the last few years I have been appearing on many television talk shows as an exercise expert, and have had the opportunity to meet many celebrities in all professions. During conversations with these people, both on and off camera, I am frequently asked for exercise advice. As a matter of curiosity, I too ask questions about the personal exercise habits of each person I meet, because I am always interested in the variety of exercises practiced by famous people.

I am a total believer in the exercise I do and teach—stretch exercise—which is the warm-up stretching that every ballet and modern dancer does before a class or performance. I was trained to be a dancer, and know first-hand that dancers' bodies are healthy, strong, graceful, and proportionate. But there are many different ways to exercise with success, depending on what type of body you have and what you want exercise to do for you.

Exercise technically means activity for the purpose of training or developing the body, which actually means moving the body for the purpose of being healthier, better able to perform a physical skill, or developing a better-looking shape. These motivations for exercise are the same for everyone, whether they are famous or not.

There are successful people in all walks of life, but this book deals only with those who are well known to everyone—celebrities. The celebrities in this book are not "body celebrities"; they are people who are more famous for themselves than for their bodies, so the exercise information is straight and not an extension of their physical image. They have nothing to gain from making their exercise habits public, except the knowledge that they may have helped other people find satisfactory, workable exercise solutions.

Famous people usually have good health, and figures that complement their success personality. They seem to achieve a total body awareness that's right for them as individuals. As Mrs. Norman Vincent Peale told me, "The body and mind interact. Your physical being telescopes constantly to your mind. One feeds and stimulates the other, and so you have a type of seesaw thing going on between body and mind with the life force as a middle balance point."

You may not be accustomed to thinking of Dr. and Mrs. Norman Vincent Peale, Lady Bird Johnson, Eleanor McGovern, Dr. Joyce Brothers, Sylvia Porter, or Art Buchwald and other celebrities in this book as "body people," but they all have very interesting, logical things to say about exercise. You can see they know what

they're talking about.

And then there are Polly Bergen, Arlene Dahl, Rita Gam, and all the others whom we've always presumed were blessed with perfect bodies but discover, when it comes right down to the truth, that their bodies are no more perfect than anyone else's. They just know what to do to diminish their imperfections. They also have some good exercise information.

It makes you wonder what this "perfect" figure is that we keep hearing about, and if there really is such a thing. There are some people—few, but some—who were born with a combination of proportionate bone and muscle structure and properly balanced metabolism, and come as close to the perfect body as is possible. But, more often than you know, the commercial cheesecake that's advertised as the perfect figure is filled with silicone and trussed with elastic.

You can rather generally divide exercise into three styles:

1 Exercise that builds muscle strength (isometrics for example)

2 Exercise that develops skill for sport (calisthenics)

3 Exercise that develops flexibility and endurance (stretch exercise)

Exercise that improves the figure usually falls in the third category, although the figure is certainly some-what improved in the process of practicing the first two types of exercise. The most ideal exercise style for improving the figure is in the grac ful physical arts such as gymnastics and dance, because all three types of exercise are combined at the same time.

Most people need exercise that is woven naturally into their day— exercise that blends with their lifestyle and helps them become flexible, healthy, and fit. This is exercise that alternately stretches and relaxes the muscles. The pleasure exercises— walking, swimming, gardening and others—exemplify this, and successful people seem to know it instinctively.

The more I asked famous people about their exercise habits, the more I began to suspect a definite relation between success and fitness. I noticed that all famous people had one thing in common—energy. Where did their energy come from? Were they born with it or did they develop it?

Was there a relation between a person's fame and his or her physical condition? Certainly energy was a factor. Was it possible that successful people had fulfilled their talent goals because they had mastered their bodies?

Some place along the line someone told me that the greatest loss of energy comes when you let your negative emotions take over, which hinders your success drive. You have to be able to stay buoyant and positive if you're going to reach your goals. Some people stay buoyant because they are motivated by the dream of success in their field. Others, like Mrs. Lyndon Johnson, find the satisfactory fulfillment of each day keeps them buoyant.

I talked to actresses, writers, musicians, politicians, business and religious leaders—men and women who knew all types of success. With few exceptions they discovered there certainly was a relationship between their fame and the fitness of their bodies. I thought the way they all arrived at this conclusion was interesting enough to create a book called *Celebrity Exercise.*

As we well know, not every famous person has that perfect body to begin with; yet, the figures they achieve tend to be right for them and part of their total personality. Don't get the idea that celebrities are exercise fanatics. In fact, the opposite is more often true. Generally they do not think of exercise as a separate function in their lives; whatever they do for exercise they seem to be able to work quite naturally into their time.

Exercise is, after all, a natural body response to the need for movement. When we hunger we eat; when we tire we sleep. When we feel dull, tired, listless, and have general aches and pains, we need exercise.

Most of the famous people I talked to are walkers. Some walk to wear off nervous energy; this type of walker is a brisk walker and burns off extra calories in the process. Some walk to see and explore, and it feels good to them and stimulates enthusiasm for their ideas and life in general. Some walk to calm themselves, either to unwind or prepare for something. Many dedicated, daily walkers do nothing more than walk, but they walk a lot. Ruth Gordon, Sylvia Porter, The Amazing Kreskin and B. B. King are walkers, for example.

Recreational exercise—swimming, tennis, golfing, skiing—serves almost as large a group. One interesting observation is that gregarious personalities (performers) tend to choose the "performing" recreational sports for exercise such as tennis and golf. Sensitive, introverted "thinkers and doers" tend to choose the less noticeable, individual recreational exercises of walking, swimming, and gardening.

Very few celebrities do the traditional calisthenics, with the exception of a few who have a specific exercise, which they do for a particular purpose and repeat on a regular basis.

Then there are the people who have devised their own routines—the imaginary tennis players who play a pretend game in their bedrooms, the imaginary golfers who make up their own exercise based on a swing, the runners because they don't have time to walk, the stretchers who sneak a good body stretch when no one's looking, and the sex advocates who are convinced that sex is the ultimate exercise for their figure, their fitness, and their fun. It's been said that sex is a great way to burn off extra calories.

The uniqueness of celebrities' exercise is that they assume a right to exercise as they choose in a way that most benefits them. They retain initiative and self-direction of their bodies. They are not victims of the exercise fads, nor do they suffer the guilt syndrome about exercise that so many people do. They are aware of their body imperfections but are not hung up on them. They do what they can to minimize their flaws, but always maximize themselves as individuals.

No two people in this world are mentally, physically, and emotionally alike. That's what makes people interesting. But everyone has in common the same basic physiological and anatomical design. The ideal to seek is maximum physical development of the body you have in the style that is most natural to you as an individual and is your own mental and emotional expression. Famous people achieve the ideal. You can too.

Celebrities are interesting people. They are under constant pressure to look and act their best, at all times, in all situations. When you consider that this is in addition to maintaining competence in their profession, you can see just how extraordinary these people are. They are the source of the most workable exercise information available, and have been most cooperative in sharing the secrets of their exercise success.

So this is a how-to book filled with wide variety of exercise information that I have culled from the famous for you to identify with and learn from—examples that coincide with your body type, profession, interests, and favorite personalities. The selection of celebrities for this book was done at random, with the idea of presenting as many types of people as possible. To make the information most effective for you, I would suggest you read it three different ways:

1  Find your particular body type in the table of contents and read that section first.

2  Then read about the celebrities who are of special interest to you.

3  After you have digested the exercise information that is of the most immediate use, read the book through so that you can get a deeper, more total understanding of the subject of exercise. There is information that applies to you in every chapter, regardless of your body type.

The exercises described should be performed according to your individual needs and in keeping with your physical abilities. I believe that each one should be repeated at least four times. However, you are the best judge of what is right for you, so let common sense be your guide.

May everybody benefit from the success of the celebrities!

# UNDER FORTY

FROM birth to forty is a long span of formative years in which a person's body goes through many changes. Some people establish lifelong exercise habits—some don't. At each decade—ten, twenty, thirty, and forty—it's easy to recognize the body that assimilates exercise in its lifestyle and the body that doesn't. The telltale signs are posture, weight distribution, and skin coloring.

At age ten a child's bone proportions are what they will be at twenty. The proportion of one part of the body to the other does not change during subsequent growth, regardless of the muscle development or fat accumulation that might disguise it.

But it's the posture, muscle development, and fat accumulation that does change and is of the most concern in developing a good, attractive figure. In order to arrive at adulthood with a good figure—and keep it—it helps to have an understanding of body alignment, because that's the basis of all figure control.

The ideal body posture (alignment) is a line of support through the center of the three main bulks of body weight —head, chest, and pelvis. From this invisible axis your body is supposed to maintain balance with an equalization of bone and muscle force. When the whole body is in correct alignment the weight can be distributed evenly.

The function of the skeleton is to support the weight of the body and protect its inner workings. The pelvis must receive, through the spinal column, the entire weight of the head, shoulders, and trunk, and distribute it to the legs. If the bones are in proper alignment they can bear an unbelievable amount of weight quite adequately, for they have the durable characteristics of steel.

And if the body is in proper alignment it is much easier to maintain a figure that is well proportioned in the relation of hips to waist to chest. It's that harmoniously proportionate body we all seek in whatever size skeletal frame we are.

The formative years to age twenty are crucial ones in basic figure formation. Figure defects can begin in youth if growing-up exercises have been insufficient. Teen-age eating habits, consisting of quantities of junk food, compound such defects by accumulating excess weight in stomach/hip areas. This misproportion of weight throughout the body creates unhealthy sluggishness, misaligns the body, and frequently sets a negative figure pattern for the future.

A young woman may not have full breast development at the same time she has extra-heavy hips, and because she is figure conscious becomes a captive audience for the commercial media, trying every novelty diet that comes along, making her problems worse. Or she might suffer because she is overdeveloped physically, but emotionally immature. It is good to know that the body is capable of change.

This changing, shaping process usually takes place quite normally for most people; for those who hit a stretch of time when the body formation is erratic it can be trying.

Arlene Dahl told me that she never had a figure until she was seventeen, and then she was a size eight on the top and a ten on the bottom. At fourteen Polly Bergen was 40-25-40. Vivian Blaine went through a terrible period of overweight at age sixteen, starving herself with liquid diets only to find out eventually that her weight problem was water retention. Rubye Graham, editor of *Seventeen* Magazine, grew up without any exercise at all. As a result, her body does not "feel" movement, and she fights a constant weight problem.

Children must grow up moving. And girls must run and jump and be involved in physical sports just like boys. After childhood, how much exercise do you need? How much is enough?

Adequate exercise is proportionate to the body's physical need and performance. The more you exercise the stronger your body becomes and the more you will be able to do. Enough exercise for one person differs from enough exercise for another person, but your body should be able to successfully perform the tasks you must do each day. You can judge your own level of exercise need by the way you look, feel, and perform. If you are not satisfied with your figure, your energy level, your health and physical ability, then your exercising is probably inadequate.

One must begin to do some real self-evaluation from thirty to forty if a healthy, attractive body is to be sustained through the middle period of life.

The celebrities that follow in this Under Forty category range in age from twenty to forty. None of them has a perfect body; yet all are interesting, successful people in which movement is a part of their lives. Since this is the starting point in the book, it seems apropos to include a few young, less well-known celebrities who are just beginning their careers. I chose them especially so I could share with you the physical struggles they've had in "taming" their figures and the success it has started to bring them.

I would like to dedicate this book to Victoria Uris, a promising modern dancer, whose approach to life—and to exercise—is a fine example to us all.

# Victoria Uris

☼ *An extraordinary young dancer*

VICTORIA URIS, when she was thirteen years old, fell in love with the dance at the Rockland Country Day School in Congers, New York. I was head of the modern dance and physical education department at the time. It was a sudden thing. After constantly cutting my classes for a variety of reasons, she came to me one day and announced that she wanted to take every class available. She had seen a performance of the Alvin Ailey Dance Company and decided she must become a modern dancer.

She was one of the last girls in the school that I would have guessed desired such a career; she had no background in dance, no inclination to it, and a rather lumbering way of moving. There were other girls in the school who were already dancing and were more obviously headed in that direction.

It was an exciting thing for me to reach a student whose dedication to dance was equal to my own. The teacher who is fortunate enough to see the dedication taken to the professional performance level is amply rewarded.

Victoria is in this book because I have never met another person who struggled so hard to "tame" her body so that she could be accepted as a dancer. She appeared large (she was only 5'6") and she carried too much weight, but it was not excessive fat that could be shed easily.

There were scholarship summers spent at Jacob's Pillow in Lee, Massachusetts, where she danced with Norman Walker's group; there was a college education earned at New York University School of the Arts; there was constant training in dance with the best teachers. All this time Victoria was turning into a very talented dancer, but never getting the bid from a professional group because she was visually too large.

She dieted, increased her exercising, dieted more, and joined the New York Dance Collective at NYU. When I was putting this book together, I saw her again in New York. After more than ten years of hard work she had the lithe body of the dancer and had just joined the Paul Taylor Modern Dance Company as an apprentice.

There is probably no one who exercises more than the dancer. The dancer is expected to have a perfect body. So in a book that is meant for people in nonmovement lives, it might seem unfair to use as an example a young person for whom exercise and body movement are a way of life. But if the dancer has the same problem as the nondancer, even with the advantage of constant exercise, isn't her solution to the problem even more valid?

Yes. And Victoria gives me the opportunity to make it very clear that body weight is an individual thing that cannot be controlled by exercise alone. It is a combination of exercise and diet and the way one's own individual body chemistry operates.

Victoria lived on a low-calorie diet in addition to doing strenuous exercise and dance; she did everything right to lose weight but she could never get below a certain point until she found out she was not getting enough iron in her diet. Even though Victoria was living the healthy life of the dancer, she did feel tired most of the time.

After she started taking extra iron, she began to lose the excess pounds. I am not enough of an expert in the field of nutrition, metabolism, and body chemistry to be able to explain why the iron made the difference, but for her it did. I have always suspected that assimilation of food is the root of many body mysteries.

I would not presume that a lack of iron is a contributing cause of other people's overweight, but it is one of the many possibilities to consider. Only your doctor can determine that.

Victoria Uris does not have any single exercise secret to pass on to you. All the dancer's exercises are part of her daily routine.

She did say to me with great joy and conviction, "Everyone should dance."

# Joan Garrity

☼ *The sensuous woman*

BOB DAVIDOFF STUDIOS

IF YOU THINK "J" does all her exercising in bed you're wrong. She's an ardent golfer and also plays tennis one hour a day. She loves to exercise as long as it doesn't seem like drudgery, for she admits she lacks the discipline needed to stick to a boring fitness program.

"J" is Joan Garrity, author of *The Sensuous Woman,* the book that surprised America a few years ago and set off a chain reaction of sensuous books in almost every category.

Joan grew up in Missouri, and has been a newspaper reporter, an actress, theatrical publicist, department store clerk, puppeteer, secretary, and book publicist. In addition to writing *The Sensuous Woman,* she co-authored a bargain-shopping guide of New York City and wrote *The Golfer's Guide to Florida Courses.*

Presently she is writing two books— a how-to book on love and *The Golfer's Guide to the Southeastern States.*

When I first found out that "J" also wrote golf books, I didn't believe it; but she is a golfer—an ardent one— and since the publication of her book and the success it has brought her, she's been able to indulge in the game of golf on a more regular basis.

She has her own little exercise ritual that she goes through several times a day to relax her and stimulate circulation: standing up straight with chin held high, feet well apart, she does a vertical swim stroke reaching for the ceiling, alternating arms twenty times each arm; then she does an imaginary backstroke for another twenty counts; to finish the swim sequence, she bends forward from the hips and does an overarm stroke twenty more times with each arm, stretching the fingers out as far as she can.

Following her imaginary swim, "J" does a golf exercise that she copied from her father. This is beneficial as an exercise, and if she doesn't get out on the course regularly it keeps her wrist and hip action from becoming stiff.

"Now if I could only think up an exercise that would cure a wicked slice, I wouldn't need an adding machine to total up my score," she said.

Her present writing schedule requires her to spend a great amount of time sitting, so her exercises are necessary tension relievers. They are also helpful in clearing her head when she hits a writing block. If you too sit for long periods of time, take a simple break like hers. It does stimulate the thinking process.

To do her golf exercise, stand with knees flexed and feet spread shoulder width, head down, weight distributed equally on both feet, and hands gripping an invisible club. Swing the legs, hips, and arms briskly from left to right, left to right, about thirty times, simulating the weight shift of a short iron shot. Then reverse the action to keep flexibility equalized.

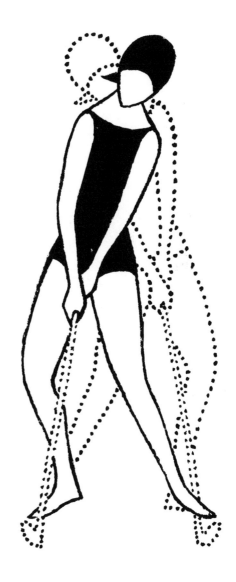

# Sheila Rabb Weidenfeld

☼ *Press secretary to Betty Ford*

From eight o'clock every morning until things are over for the day at the White House, Sheila is on duty—accessible to both Mrs. Ford and all the people who want to learn about, interview, and meet the President's wife. She works in her office all day, attends social functions, and travels with the First Lady. She loves her job.

Sheila is from Massachusetts and attended Brandeis University. When her husband took a position in Washington a few years ago she landed a job producing the "Panorama Show," a television show that had been limping along with poor ratings. Through her efforts, she helped make it the major Washington television show it is today. She never expected to go from television to the White House, but is glad it happened.

"I think about my figure every once in a while, because I have no time to exercise and wonder what's happening to my body."

Sheila is 5'2" and weighs about

$A$T THE beginning of the Ford Administration, Betty Ford put out a call along the grapevine for a press secretary. The woman most frequently recommended to her was Sheila Rabb Weidenfeld. Sheila got the job and Mrs. Ford got herself a prize. She is a pleasant, quick, bright, extremely capable young woman.

102 pounds. There is no visible figure fault, nor does she seem to be suffering from her lack of exercise, because she does all the things any successful, interesting, happy person does; she moves.

She moves constantly. She walks everywhere, runs up and down stairs, and loves to dance. She didn't realize she was getting good exercise that way until I pointed it out to her and quoted what Pauline Trigère, the dress designer, had said to me: "I am exercising all the time without knowing because I am not a static person."

Sheila is an exceptionally vibrant person and her body absorbs, uses, and restimulates itself with its own energy. She unconsciously uses a style of body control that also controls her figure. When she is at her desk, she sits the same way dancers sit, as Marian McPartland, the jazz pianist sits, slightly forward and off the buttocks so that her weight is evenly distributed and she is able to move quickly from any position. Even when she leans back in her chair, she doesn't let her total weight drop to her hips.

It's a type of invisible control many people have that keeps a figure in good shape. Anyone can learn it just by understanding it. Dancers know it. Models know it. Sheila uses it. Any graceful exercise you do that requires muscle control for the fluidity of the movement will help develop it.

Try this one. Stand in good posture, weight held as high as possible, and bend the knees slightly. Return to standing position and pull up your entire body to a half toe position. Hold briefly, tighten stomach/buttocks muscles and repeat slowly four times, holding weight high throughout and moving fluidly.

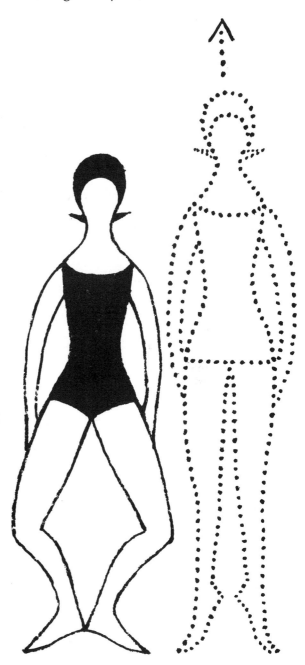

# Barbara Blazie

☼ *A rising young fashion mode*
*and actress*

MANY actresses reach the stage through modeling, which is what Barbara Blazier has done—although she didn't plan it that way. She had no idea that she would ever be considered model material since she is very healthy looking—not willowy and gaunt. She's a large girl (5'9") with a tendency to put on weight easily.

But it was that healthy American-girl look that came through when she was first discovered by *Seventeen* Magazine. Since then she has become more and more in demand as a photographic model and is doing television commercials in addition to her acting.

Barbara was raised in Larchmont, New York, and went to Lawrence University in Appleton, Wisconsin, or an academic scholarship, directly from her junior year in high school. But her love for the theater was strong and she left college after the first year to study acting at the famed Neighborhood Playhouse in New York City. She has since been seen in a variety of experimental and traditional theatrical productions off Broadway.

"I think of exercise more as a way to relax than as a way to keep a decent figure. Tension can ruin a stage performance, and I've noticed that it comes across to the photographer, too. Exercise relieves my tension," she told me.

For general exercise and good health she does all kinds of movements. Yoga is her favorite form; she takes a class twice a week, and credits it with the control of her figure. She walks a lot, rather than taking a cab or bus, and whenever she's alone during the day she does some kind of exercise—usually the stretch exercises because they're best for proportioning. With her type of build she's discovered that if she keeps her body in proportion, any extra weight she may be carrying doesn't really show.

Barbara has a favorite exercise that she loves because it's very relaxing, revitalizing, and most of all, tension-relieving. She compares the whole feeling of the exercise to the way a thermometer works, with the mercury rising, then falling. As she bends over to touch the floor, the "mercury" is forced to the top of her head and fingertips, and as she returns to position the "mercury" falls.

To do her thermometer exercise, stand with feet about twelve inches apart. Raise your arms overhead, and then stretch all the way down to touch the floor in front of you, lingering about six seconds until you feel the pull up the backs of your legs and the blood rush to your head. Then slowly stretch your body back up to its starting point, concentrating on each segment of your spine as you return to a straight, but uplifted position.

Barbara does this exercise four times each morning after rising and four times each evening before she retires. If tension is a problem for you, too, try it.

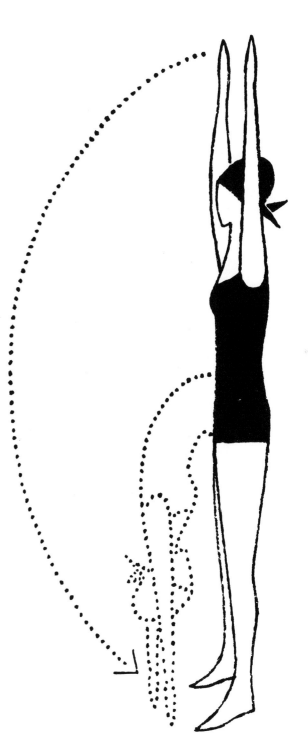

# Gladys Knight and the Pips

☼ *A dynamite pop/rock vocal group*

Georgia, Gladys has been performing since she was four years old. When she was seven she won the grand prize on Ted Mack's Amateur Hour. Her parents were singers in the famed Wings Over Jordan Choir. When she was twelve years old, she and the group won an amateur contest in Atlanta, and that launched them on their successful career.

For the sake of her own health, and also because of her appearances with the Pips, Gladys is very diet and exercise conscious. For her, regular weekly attendance at an exercise spa is best. She feels she needs a definite, directed exercise routine, and is faithful to it. She has no particular favorite exercise; she concedes she simply feels and looks best when she follows the total exercise session at her spa.

That total exercise session usually begins with a half hour's worth of machine exercising that helps her to strengthen her body with weights and pulleys. She then gets about a half hour of exercise instruction, which is a blend of calisthenics and dance-type exercises.

THIS family group consists of Gladys Knight, singer, and the Pips: her brother Merald Jr., and their cousins Edward Patten and William Guest. They started performing together as children. Born in Atlanta,

If, from week to week, her stomach, hips, or any other part of her body gets slightly out of proportion, she does spot exercising to work off the excess. This usually means extra time spent on one of the machines or concentrated exercising on a mat or slant board.

The Pips get their exercise playing basketball. This does it for them. They play frequently with their own and with the neighborhood kids, and thoroughly enjoy the physical involvement in the game. It keeps them trim and flexible, and besides that it's fun. It's a very good way for them to balance their performing schedule with recreation and exercise, and provides them with the opportunity to spend much enjoyable time with their youngsters.

Basketball and other team sports provide physical activity that involves relating to other people, and is also an enjoyable way of keeping fit. You're physically forced to practice consideration and cooperation, control and respect, and at the same time move skillfully—a well-ordered total body/mind involvement. More tangible physical benefit is in healthier heart action, better muscle endurance, and body coordination.

The opportunities for men to indulge in a team sport after leaving school are slim. Yet, anyone who really enjoys a game like basketball should be able to round up enough men (or boys) with similar interest and put together an adequate team situation.

Even if you only do a little dribbling and basket shooting in the neighborhood, you're doing something. I would suggest a little short-distance jogging for conditioning (you could jog to the bus stop in the morning). It's good for your heart and it develops some of the balance you'll need in any sport. Spend two minutes jogging in the beginning, and extend the time according to your individual needs.

# Robert Kahn

☼ *Leading dancer with the Paul Taylor Company*

Most people see exercise as an external group of movements that are done to improve circulation, burn off extra calories, and develop specific groups of muscles. This is valid, but there is further exercise ability and effectiveness that comes from within the body as muscles reach out for strength instead of tightening into set positions.

ONE of the reasons a dancer like Robert Kahn becomes so strong, without looking like a Tarzan, is because of the stretching exercises he does. He must be able to move gracefully from one position to another with complete control, whether the movement sequence calls for a leap, a series of turns, or any other feat of technical virtuosity. This calls for an unusual amount of flexible strength.

The dancer, therefore, exercises from within the body for total control, and develops strength, grace, flexibility, endurance, and good health—an ideal of body use.

Stretch exercise differs from calisthenics, isometrics, aerobics (exercises that bring air into the body), and other forms because it is a process of stretching, relaxing, stretching, relaxing away from the body until weight becomes more evenly distributed and muscles reach their maximum strength. The more traditional styles of exercise concentrate on stationary and locomotor development of the body as it is, achieving muscle strength but not as much elasticity. There is very little danger of injuring the body through stretch exercising because any sensation of pain acts as a restraint. Thus tight, stiff muscles are not overstretched.

Yet, the one problem Robert told me he had was an overstretched right side, the result of a very common practice we're all guilty of—favoring one side with extra exercise. This is the side that corresponds to the hand you use for writing. It's probably something you've never thought of, but the hand you write with opens every door and takes the first step, and when a young dancer exercises, practices difficult movements, or learns a new combination, he or she is inclined to learn it and perfect it on the easier side; this eventually shows and causes problems that must be corrected.

Robert Kahn dances with the famous Paul Taylor Modern Dance Company. He grew up in the Detroit area and attended Cranbrook Academy. Ice hockey was his love; he played goalie. But one day he watched a dance class, decided to study dance, and ultimately made it his profession.

it will take a few sessions to stretch those tight muscles. But in time, you will. Do this exercise four times on each side. Just remember to do both sides equally, so one doesn't become overstretched in relation to the other.

Some athletes use a group of stretching exercises devised for the dance. The one that is used by the Los Angeles Rams to stretch the groin and hamstring muscles is a good one for any pro or amateur athlete to do. Prop your leg securely on a stationary object (the dancer would do this at the ballet barre) and stretch as closely as possible, head to knee. In the beginning don't expect to do it as well as the picture demonstrates, because

# FORTY TO SIXTY

THERE is a natural relationship between who and what people are and how and why they move their bodies. If you try to separate the physical from the mental, you lose the personality of the person. It's that individual blending of the physical and mental that makes each person interesting. This is something that becomes manifest in people from the age of forty. It is obvious in celebrities because in order to protect themselves and their talents, they must be aware of themselves as total human beings.

For instance, visualize Sammy Davis Jr. and B. B. King; Sammy is light, loud, and moves constantly as he performs; B. B. King is round, quiet, and usually sits as he sings. Can you imagine these two men in each other's bodies? They wouldn't be able to be who they are.

Elinor Ross, the opera singer, and Marian McPartland, the jazz pianist, are about the same height, but there's about fifty pounds difference in their weights. Yet, both are healthy and have figures that are completely right for them. Elinor, who has a beautiful dramatic soprano voice, talks and moves slowly; Marian talks fast and moves quickly.

This book has a triple purpose: first, to interest you in exercise; second, to offer examples of famous people whose body type, interests in life and exercise needs correspond to your own, and third, to illustrate specific exercises within each body type that can be done to eliminate various problem areas.

Viscerally, it's a wonder many of us survive this long when you consider the abuses we inflict on our bodies— alcohol, food excess, and smoking, for example. If we are in good general condition and the abuses are not constant, our bodies handle them quit well. Serious physical problems often emerge around the age of forty because of stress and strain in both ou professional and family life. If you understand your body, it's much easie to control the external forces that do damage to it internally.

Think of your body as a living machine. People and machines both need fuel as a source of energy, and that energy is used to produce heat and perform work. Waste products must be eliminated. Specific parts of the body have specialized functions, and the failure of one part may cause a breakdown of the entire machine.

The food you eat supplies your energy. Only 15 percent of your total energy is available to you for conscious use. Heart action and other unconscious functions use the other 85 percent. When your body processes deteriorate through improper health habits, sickness, or abuse, they must draw energy from that 15 percent that you use for the conscious purposes of working, thinking, and so on. But in times of stress, you draw energy from the other 85 percent that is involved in unconscious processes.

That's why stress is so debilitating if allowed to continue for long periods. Even in sleep, your body is reacting to daytime stress.

The human body is a self-healing organism when it is properly maintained. It is a living unit that renews itself at the rate of three billion cells a minute. It is more miraculous than a machine, for it is self-operating and self-repairing; it grows, repro-duces, adapts; it can alter itself, have an environmental awareness, have purpose and foresight.

Machines can be fixed quite easily when they wear out; the human body cannot. So it's wise to exercise and keep it in good working condition. If you have been unable to sustain any regular exercise plan, it is because you have not found a movement style that has kept your interest or was right for you. Consciously or subconsciously,

the brain controls everything the body does, and if the body is not doing meaningful exercise the brain cannot sustain a governing interest in it.

The quality that stands out the most in celebrity exercise is the initiative of famous, successful people to do what they want about exercise instead of what they think they are supposed to do. They do what interests them and are therefore able to stay with it.

Many people from forty to sixty are guilt-ridden about their lack of interest in exercising. They need not be. The best advice I can give you is to keep trying until you find the right style of movement. Have you considered archery, badminton, handball, squash, dancing, fencing, boating, bowling, fishing, gardening, hang gliding, hiking, ice skating, judo, swimming, table tennis, T'ai Chi Ch'uan, paddle tennis?

It is never too late to begin exercising. You don't have to spend the rest of your life feeling under par, wearing an unattractive body, and suffering from nonidentity.

# Frankie Hewitt

☼ *Washington's prominent theatrical producer*

"My BODY must move a certain amount each day or I feel incomplete. So I walk in preference to riding, whenever possible. In Ford's Theater in Washington, D.C., where I have my office, there are stairs connecting each room, so I walk, and sometimes run, to discuss something with one of my assistants rather than ask them to come into my office. I am five feet nine inches tall, have weighed the same amount since I was sixteen, and wear a perfect size twelve."

Frankie Hewitt's greatest fame came with the transformation of Ford's Theater from an antiquated Lincoln Museum to a living theater, a feat for which both tourists and Washingtonians will be eternally grateful.

Here is what actually happened. One night at a theater she and her husband, CBS Producer Don Hewitt, ran into Stewart Udall who was then Secretary of the Interior, and she suggested the idea to him. He was interested and did the necessary legislative work to make it possible. Within three years it was a reality, and Frankie was president of a nonprofit theater group providing good American drama in an historic American theater. One of the greatest hits was the play about Harry Truman called *Give 'em Hell, Harry* starring James Whitmore.

On January 30, 1968, Ford's Theater put on its first play since 1865. This made it an active, living memorial to Abraham Lincoln, who was shot there April 14, 1865, by John Wilkes Booth during a performance of *Our America*

*Cousin.* Frankie claimed that as an antiquated Lincoln Museum it was more of a memorial to the assassin than to the president. So now, more than one hundred yeras later, living theater has returned and it is indeed an impressive way of memorializing Abraham Lincoln.

Frankie was born in the Oklahoma Dust Bowl in the middle of the Depression. Her family migrated to the Napa Valley in California, where she picked grapes and prunes till she was fifteen and then left home. At seventeen she was a woman's editor of a newspaper, at nineteen an assistant advertising and publicity director at Rose Marie Reid swimsuit company, at twenty-three a political speechwriter. She has also been the head of a Senate Investigating Committee and Adlai Stevenson's assistant when he was ambassador to the United Nations.

When Frankie told me that her body must move a certain amount each day or she felt incomplete, she was referring to the total human need for movement, which is physical and emotional. This is true for all people, but few perceive it because it's intangible. "I think the nervous system, especially if it's under stress, needs the relief that exercise can give it. I don't think it has to be a particular kind of exercise, but walking or moving the body around does provide a healthy continuity for the nervous system that can mean emotional stability. I like Yoga for similar reasons. In Yoga you can have that continuity of movement in a formalized style."

Here is a Yoga "Kneeling Position" you can do once a day that will aid in digestion, give you a sense of lightness, relax you, and sharpen your mind. Hold the pose as long as you feel comfortable—at least several minutes.

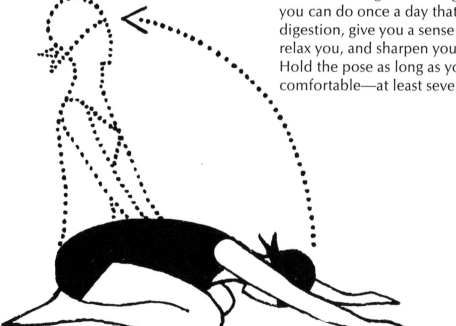

# Rita Gam

☼ *An award-winning actress of many talents*

"IF YOU'RE healthy there's no reason to ignore exercise. And if you're not feeling well, exercise can make you feel better. Even in a hospital bed, if you allow yourself to give up on exercise, you can become part of the bed. I know."

Rita's done a lot of hospital volunteer work, and has observed with interest the differences in patients and their recuperation. "If nothing else," she continued, "you can always do simple breathing exercises for your unconscious muscles while lying in bed. And there's usually always some part of your body that you can move a bit without straining anything."

She's right. Of course, use your common sense, and don't overdo. You can usually tell if you are straining yourself. The rule of thumb is: if it hurts, it's not good for you; don't do If it feels all right, it probably *is* all right. Check with your doctor if you are uncertain about pushing yourself too far.

Rita Gam has starred in eighteen movies. In 1964 she won the Best Movie Actress award for *The Silver Bear* at the Berlin International Film Festival. She has done Broadway shows, and has also been seen on such television programs as "Klute" and "Mannix."

Many years of ballet went in to Rita's training for the theater, and it shows. She continues to take one ball class a week, and goes to a gym once a week. She also does Yoga and enjoy ice skating—all total body movement that keeps proportions in good balance.

Rita says that her figure problems are legs that are too muscular and bones that are too large, very broad shoulders and a flat chest, but none of these faults are visible because she has an interesting, rather feline way of moving that captures the attention: it's graceful, flowing and totally coordinated.

It was probably that very flexible way of moving that helped her work out a serious back strain she experienced as a result of standing incorrectly during the six-month run of a play. By lying on the floor on her back and moving her legs with knees together from side to side, she was eventually able to correct the strain that had been quite painful and could have developed into something permanent.

Every morning she does five minutes worth of exercise for specific body spots. Like most people, she has to pay attention to certain spots of weight accumulation. She's 5'7" and weighs 125 pounds, and because of her well-balanced routine her weight doesn't fluctuate much.

Her favorite exercise is the bicycle, because it's "easy to do anyplace." She even does it on her bed, which I don't really recommend because of the danger of falling off the edge. If you want to use the bicycle exercise for general body conditioning, lie down on the rug on the floor to do it. For best results do it as Rita and the dancers do, pushing your buttocks as high in the air as possible at the beginning, and then reaching with pointed toes very slowly with fully extended legs toward the ceiling. This provides better action for the stomach muscles than you will get if you simply push up in the air haphazardly and spin your legs. Complete the cycle at least eight times.

# Adelle Rasey Sardi

☼ *Activist in the field of world nutrition*

**B**EING married to Vincent Sardi, the New York restaurateur, does **not** mean one overeats and becomes obese. On the contrary, his former wife Adelle Rasey is very trim. She eats well, but with refined taste, and tends to order a fresh, well-prepared fish instead of a steak.

The only imperfection in her figure is her legs. "From my knees to my ankles, I'm three-fourths of an inch too short. Actually, it isn't that serious a problem because most people don't even notice, especially when I wear high heels."

Adelle was born in Montana. At fifteen she went to Los Angeles to model and work in films before going east to New York where she began a varied career of singing and acting. She's raised four children and is now deeply involved in food philosophy and world nutrition. She is doing extensive research, trying to determine the most nutritious diets that can be developed for the entire world— cheaply and sensibly—that will help to compensate for food shortages. Ordinarily, the evolution from the theater to world nutrition would seem disconnected, but not when you realize that Adelle Rasey Sardi spent quite a few years hanging around good food.

Adelle has two specific body exercises she does daily: the first one she does for her "imperfect legs." (1) Lie on your left side, lift right leg up at a right angle to the body, turn the foot in sharply, lower the leg, and relax the foot. Lift each leg twenty times. (2) For torso flexibility, firm thigh and buttocks muscle tone, and a general feeling of well-being assume crouch position, extend your leg high to the back and return to a crouch position. Repeat ten times on each side.

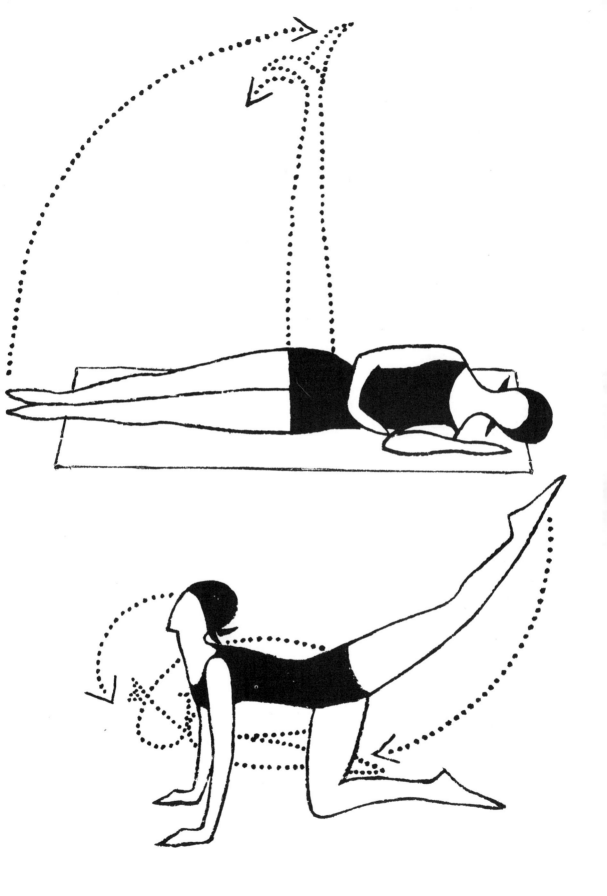

# Betty Ford

☼ *Our vivacious First Lady*

O F ALL the president's wives in the last five administrations, Betty Ford comes across to me as the one most in tune with exercise. Lady Bird Johnson is an exercise advocate and practices it every day; Jackie Kennedy Onassis is known to be very physically active, and participates in many recreational sports, as well as working out at an exclusive gym in New York City. But Betty Ford is the first one who seems to consider exercise a normal, everyday part of life. It's a pleasure to be able to include her in this book because body movement is a normal, everyday part of life, and having the First Lady confirm this belief is especially gratifying.

She has a bit of an edge on most women, however, because of her years of dance training. Those of you who have also had dance training know that body discipline becomes a lifetime habit. Her training was in modern dance, and began in Grand Rapids, Michigan. She continued to study dance at Bennington College, and was also a student with Martha Graham.

Every morning Betty Ford exercises for ten minutes. She has no restrictions, except for the tempering of any movement that might aggravate a neck/back sensitivity to osteoarthritis. She walks and swims for pleasure exercise. One reason she has maintained such a slim figure is attributed to the fact that she is aware of what she eats and stays away from fried foods and desserts; there is no in-between meal eating either.

I decided she was really aware of the importance of exercise when she said, "Standing at attention for a state arrival is great exercise; you've got everything pulled together." Even though the rest of the women in America aren't called upon to do that, the same physical discipline can be applied to any social situation that calls for total physical composure. And it eventually becomes a habit that reflects physical poise. That's something the wife of every president has learned, and it shows.

For this book, Betty Ford has given me instructions on how to "get everything pulled together," like the First Lady does. It's based on good posture, which is most important to her.

You'd be surprised how well your body will obey when your brain gives it the right directives. In this case you use mental imagery; when walking or standing, think of yourself as a puppet hanging from a string. "Everything falls into line," Mrs. Ford said. "Stretch as tall as you can, pulling your stomach in and up—toward the rib cage—and tuck in your buttocks." The result is a feeling of body lightness that is "like a string that is pulling from your head through your body, and you feel like your feet are barely touching the ground."

On an even more practical level, Mrs. Ford says the time spent under the hair dryer is most valuable for pulling in stomach muscles and lifting the rib cage. This good posture position promotes physical poise, and makes good use of your time.

Whenever you have the time (preferably every morning), do this simple stretching exercise. Stand in good posture with feet apart; reach for the ceiling very slowly and easily so that your body can feel every part of the upward motion. Keep the movement very smooth, and reach a maximum, uplifted position before returning to starting posture. But when you return to the original position, keep the body uplifted and retain the feeling of the stretch as long as you can. One time, done in very slow motion is sufficient, but go ahead and repeat it two or three more times if you choose. Each day your correct posture will be strengthened, and eventually you too will be able to "pull everything together."

# Craig Claiborne

☼ *World-renowned food edito[r]*
The New York Times

AS FOOD news editor of *The New York Times* Craig Claiborne is a cook-writer. He tours the restaurants of the world and then writes about them. His articles are syndicated to four hundred newspapers in the United States and foreign countries. He has written seven cookbooks, which have been translated into seventeen languages. Before he became food news editor he wrote the *Craig Claiborne Journal* for two years, a newsletter full of recipes and related food philosophy. For fourteen years, he had been the food critic of *The New York Times*, a position that had never before been held by a man.

Craig Claiborne was born and raised in Mississippi. Before he arrived at his fame in the culinary arts, he had tried pre-med at Mississippi A & M, studied journalism at the University of Missouri, served in the United States Navy, did public relations work in Chicago, and attended the Swiss Hotelkeeper's Association School in Lausanne, Switzerland.

His taste in food is, of course, superb. But he eats modestly and weighs 158 pounds. "Modest eating is something everyone should learn; m[ost] people eat far too much," he says. Overeating actually diminishes the pleasure of eating good food. He believes that you can get fatter eating bad food than good food. If you carry this to its logical conclusion you'll see quite clearly that you actually save money preparing good food if you eat in moderation. At the same time you will keep body fat down.

"I have done eighty to a hundred sit-ups every morning for the past two years," Craig said, "although I can't see that it has made a great difference in the contour of my abdomen, which was the reason for the exercise in the first place. On the other hand, I wonder what my profile would look like without the daily torture."

His profile would, most likely, be less trim, and his energy level would not be as high.

Many exercise specialists are saying that push-ups and sit-ups are more hazardous to the body than helpful—that they create too much body strain, especially past the age of twenty-five, and are hard on the blood pressure. There is some validity to this, especially if you are a middle-aged man or woman who has led a sedentary life since the days of school calisthenics, and are just beginning an exercise program. But if your body is used to sit-ups and you like doing them, there is no reason to stop. They certainly do tighten up the front torso muscles of the body, even though they aren't much fun.

But for those of you who cannot "stomach" sit-ups, or if Craig Claiborne wanted to vary his daily routine, here is an excellent exercise that could serve the same purpose:

Stand with feet apart. With a little give in the knees, bend as far back as is comfortable—to a point where you are still in control of your balance. Straighten, making the muscles on the front of your torso pull you back up to position. Do this eight times.

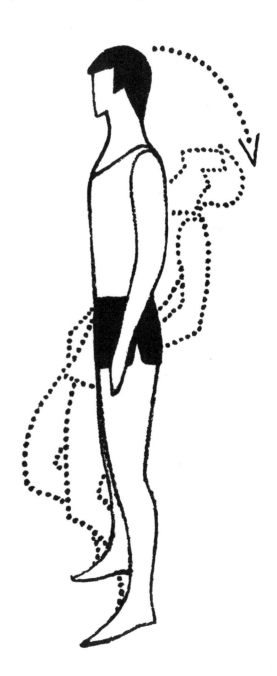

# Monty Hall

☼ *Let's Make a Deal's
sparkling emcee*

ONE OF the most popular and longest running game shows on television is "Let's Make a Deal," with Monty Hall as master of ceremonies. It's the show where people dress in outlandish costumes for the opportunity of being chosen contestants and competing for fabulous prizes. The show has made Monty Hall a celebrity, and he's recently written a book called *Emcee Monty Hall*, in which he tells of the trials and tribulations of making it in the entertainment world.

He was born Monte Halparin in Winnepeg, Canada, but he shortened his name along the career trail. He's the father of three children, and he and his wife, Marilyn, have been happily married for more than twenty-seven years.

If you've watched "Let's Make a Deal," you'll realize just how in tune Monty has to be. It's an active show for him, and he has to maintain his physical well-being to carry it off. Exercise plays a large part in maintaining his energy level.

A great part of his attention to body care is found in recreational exercise. He plays golf and tennis, both popular games among entertainment people in California who have the weather on their side for year-round play. Pleasure exercise such as golf and tennis, indulged in fairly regularly, can do much to maintain a good outlet for working off the nervous energy built up during his lively show.

Monty is 5'11" and weighs 165 pounds. He doesn't have any serious inclination to overweight, and stays about the same all the time. This is because he has a simple but effective exercise routine that he goes through twice a day.

It begins in bed in the morning before rising with a warm-up exercise that wakes up the entire body. It's an exercise that conditions the abdominal muscles and the neck muscles—a real waker-upper.

Any man who lets his abdominal muscles get flabby is subject to poor posture that results in a most unattractive body profile. Weak abdominal muscles allow the internal organs to drop, and as a result the stomach protrudes, the pelvis tilts forward, and the curve of the lower back becomes accentuated, leading to lower back pain. Such a protruding stomach (or paunch) upsets the center

of gravity in the body; as it pulls the man forward he compensates by leaning backward, bending his knees slightly and increasing the curve of his back. This is what produces the "old man's stance."

So here's Monty's exercise to maintain control of the abdomen. Lying on your back with arms folded across your chest, bring one knee as close as possible to the forehead, using the neck muscles to lift the head and meet the knee. Return to starting position. Then do the same with the other knee. Continue, alternating one knee at a time, eight times. The back muscles benefit from this exercise; the forced use of the stomach muscles insures a flatter stomach.

Monty follows this with a few sit-ups, and always does the standard toe-touching exercise while he takes his shower. The standard toe-touching exercise that we were all taught in

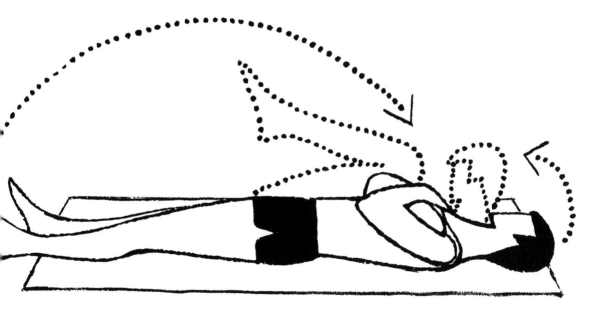

school is usually done by standing with feet together, bending forward from the waist, and trying to touch the toes.

However, unless you are a very long-waisted person, you may never be able to touch your toes in this position, and if you persist you will only strain your back and possibly do yourself some damage. That's because in a stance where the feet are together there is very little leverage left to work with from the lower back. To touch your toes you should bend forward from the waist with the help of your entire spine.

Men and women will benefit from doing this exercise with feet spread about eighteen inches apart—wider if you are over six feet tall. Reach for the floor in front of you rather than the toes, thereby "unlocking" your lower spine and allowing yourself to develop a flexible stretch. Do this four times. At a later time, when your body becomes more conditioned and better proportioned, you can do this exercise with legs together if you choose. However, I would always suggest working in the bigger, more open movement first for better body flexibility.

"Like many people these days, I am conscious of the dangers of our sedentary living, and I try to compensate by getting as much extra exercise as I can," Monty said. One of the most pleasant ways he's found to get extra exercise easily, and combat his concern for our inactive lives, is by taking advantage of spontaneous opportunities for extra body movement

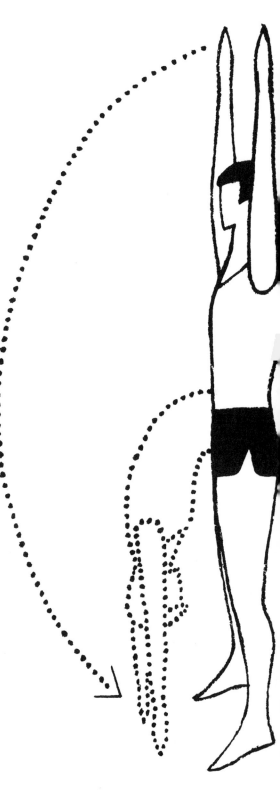

such as romping on the beach with his youngest daughter, Sharon.

The beach is a great place to get exercise. So is the back yard. Go outside and play with your kids—or inside. It's fun and it's good for all of you. There is hidden exercise value in body play, because when a person becomes happy and relaxed the tight, tense muscles give way to further relaxation and more flexibility. The oxygen supply to the cells is better, a more healthy body circulation results, muscle use is more even, and the final feeling of fatigue is physically satisfying.

If you don't stand a chance of being a contestant on "Let's Make a Deal" and winning fabulous prizes, try Monty Hall's exercise plan so you can at least feel fabulous. The greatest prize in life is continued good health.

# William Proxmire

☼ *The physically fit Senator from Wisconsin*

SENATOR William Proxmire, Democrat of Wisconsin, who is well known for his interest in physical fitness, wrote a book on exercise called *You Can Do It*. I keep up with the exercise books in print and read this one with enthusiasm. I learned from the Senator's book lots of things that everyone can do for exercise if they just keep a stiff upper lip and *do it*. But I never found out in reading the book exactly what *he* does for exercise, or if it was possible that he actually did everything in the book that he would have the readers do. This is what he told me.

"Each morning I do about twenty-five minutes of calisthenics—including one hundred push-ups, one hundred combination sit-ups and leg lifts, and a series of other exercises. In addition to that, I either run five miles or pedal ten miles on a stationary bicycle; or, in the summer, swim a mile. Each is equivalent. Normally I get six or seven days of this kind of aerobic exercise and never miss a day—three hundred sixty-five days a year—doing my calisthenics."

A few years ago an Air Force doctor developed a system of exercise called Aerobics. This was the result of research that proved that the best exercises for human fitness are those that bring in the most oxygen to all areas of the body. Oxygen, combined with other body processes, produces energy. Extensive study determined that those forms of exercise that bring in the most oxygen are: running, swimming, cycling, walking, stationary running, handball, basketball and squash. Note that with the exception of running and stationary running they're all forms of pleasure exercise.

Senator Proxmire has done his calisthenics since he was fourteen years old. Ten years ago he added running to his regimen. Now that he's also doing aerobic exercise he's noticed a more relaxed and comfortable body tone throughout the day and a somewhat greater degree of mental alertness. That's probably because of the increased oxygen intake that stimulates the brain cells.

(Incidentally, psychiatrists will frequently recommend exercise—especially at waking—to combat morning depression. Plenty of extra exercise is good for treating emotional problems in general because it tends to replace negative energy with positive energy.)

"I have a slender build— one hundred fifty-five pounds, six feet tall— with no particular body imperfections or physical impairments." Could anybody have body imperfections or physical impairments after all that exercise he does?

Go ahead—*you can do it!*

As a starter, try a partial sit-up, as shown below. Lie on the floor, raise your body from the waist up to a sitting position; return to the floor. Do this four times, at least.

And then think about the aerobic exercise concept. If it does for you what it does for Senator Proxmire, it may be just what you need.

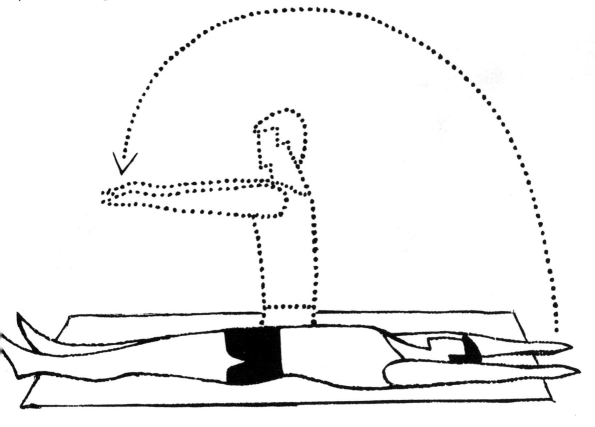

# Alan King

☼ *A multi-talented writer and comic*

"I CAN give a six-word discourse on the subject of exercise: I play tennis for exercise, period."

He wished he could offer more on the subject, but Alan King said tennis is the extent of his exercise and he regards it as a sport, not a physical fitness regimen.

Little did he realize he was just one more celebrity proving one of the major points of this book—that very few people actually involve themselves in what we've been taught is a physical fitness regimen (gymnasium workouts, self-imposed calisthenics, and other routines) but every celebrity does have something he or she does by choice, which actually amounts to exercise.

Some people might debate whether or not tennis, or any other recreational sport, can actually substitute as exercise; yet, physical movement in sport *is* exercise, and I have yet to meet a tennis player who is not much healthier than a nontennis player who doesn't have a specific physical fitness regimen either.

My reply to Alan King was seven words on the subject of exercise: better than nothing, you should play tennis.

Alan King was born Irwin Alan Kniberg on December 26, 1927, in New York. He started in show business at fifteen with a four-man band and then switched to comedy. During the sixties he became known as a supper club comic entertainer and made his stage debut in 1965 as Nathan Detroit in a New York City Center revival of *Guys and Dolls*. He also did *The Impossible Years* on Broadway and *Bye, Bye, Braverman* for the movies. He is the author of two books—*Anyone Who Owns His Own Home Deserves It* and *Help! I'm a Prisoner in a Chinese Bakery*. He's married to the former Jeannette Sprung and is the father of two sons and a daughter.

Just in case Alan decides to do

himself and his game of tennis a favor, here is an exercise that I recommend. Actually, it's a good general exercise for all men and women, borrowed from the Los Angeles Rams for whom I have a special feeling ever since two of their coaches named me an Honorary Left Guard!

Stand in good posture, legs well spread. As the diagram shows, do ten full circles for each body area designated—neck, shoulders, and trunk. Do it every morning before dressing. Don't tighten up; do it in a relaxed manner, slowly. It won't make any dramatic changes in your body, but it will loosen your muscles. A brief warm-up every morning will make you feel better throughout the day.

Do it also after a game of tennis to relieve the muscular tension of the game.

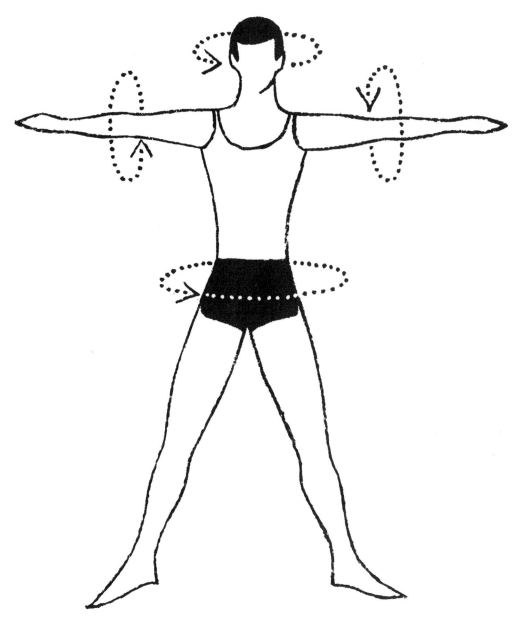

# OVER SIXTY

YOUR BODY is like a well-made machine; if kept in good use and cared for it will last a lifetime. If you ignore its maintenance over a long period of time it will rust, grow sluggish, and lose its strength, flexibility, and endurance.

The body muscle tone does show some deterioration at sixty plus, and if you haven't been used to a regular exercise program to maintain your muscle tone, it can be a great factor in debilitation. People who don't exercise at all use more muscle energy just maintaining the sedentary positions of sitting or standing than people who do exercise. Inactivity deteriorates the body cumulatively. Wherever there is muscle, there is need for movement.

Because of our intellectual, mechanized society our body movements are confined to our occupational style. We have very little opportunity to bend and stretch, other than to pick up things. If you add this to the fact that there are a large group of people who retire around sixty, you can see that the prospect of continuing exercise is an important consideration for good health. The problem is that many people don't realize how important!

This is a negative way to start a chapter in which the celebrity examples are all positive, healthy, exercising people, but in an age group where too many people use their age as an excuse to be inactive, I think it's important to underscore the dangers of inactivity right here at the beginning. Then, together with Helen Hayes, Ruth Gordon, Jan Peerce, and the Norman Vincent Peales, I can offer some logical exercise solutions.

The first sensible reaction is to turn to the basic natural body movements that are found in the daily motions of waking up, getting out of bed, sitting, standing, and walking. You can teach yourself to utilize these natural motions as good exercise by learning to involve your entire body in them. This will assure you a minimal level of daily exercise.

Upon waking, breathe deeply and stretch to maximum in every direction. Stretching in bed is an impulse that should be heeded because it forces, without danger, stimulation to every muscle in the body and brings a goodly supply of oxygen into the system resulting in good body circulation. It is far better to stretch slowly in the morning than it is to do vigorous calisthenics anyway. The body must be awakened with consideration, and warmed up gently.

Continue the warm-up stretching in various directions while sitting at the side of the bed. Stand up and continue stretching in all directions and reaching to maximum height. The upward stretching should have an uplifting psychological effect.

A few seconds spent in front of the mirror, moving the head forward and back, to each side, and around in a circle, can smooth the waking process even more and help align the head, neck, and spine.

Analyze the way you put on your clothes in the morning. Quite probably all your arm and leg motion is separated from the trunk. Yet, if you pulled on socks or stockings with one movement going vertically through your whole body instead of just using your hands and feet you would be strengthening your entire muscular system daily without doing anything special. Vertical strength is important for good body alignment.

Try it. Pull your knee up slightly, reach for your foot, pull on the stockings with your arms as your leg goes into the garment with a pushed movement that pulls the muscles right through your torso.

You can't beat the shower for an efficient, well-ordered opportunity to exercise. Stretch as you stand in the warm water; inhale, reach for the ceiling, and stretch your body upward, one hand and then the other, alternately, four times, exhaling when you return to your starting position.

If you do that much natural exercise every morning, you will feel noticeably better.

In various parts of the body there might be sagging. This is most noticeable in women in the neck and upper arms. Sagging necks and arms benefit from any exercise in which these muscles are used. A proud uptilt to the head does wonders, too. If you stay healthy and feel good, the feeling of pride in self sets a permanent uptilt to the head. Bodies that sag more than others show a loss of physical pride.

As we grow older the body tends to go downward. When you let go of the youthful uplift to the shoulders and rib cage, the rest of the body goes, too. The waistline catches it and begins to fill in; the stomach, having no other place to go, protrudes, putting increased strain on the lower stomach muscles that give way under the extra weight and are unable to hold it up any more, which makes the hips and buttocks fill out. The weight then placed on the thighs, legs, and feet is way out of balance. By this time the entire body is thrown so far out of alignment that it is vulnerable to anatomical and visceral problems. These are very real problems that detract from good health and an attractive appearance, but they're all problems that can be dealt with and corrected.

# Helen Hayes

✿ *The legendary First Lady of the Theater*

"**I** WAS very much guarded—much protected against injury and illness in my childhood. I guess I'd have to say that habits of careful living were so established when I was very young that when I grew up and was on my own I automatically continued to live that way. I have always taken good care of myself, observed a very strict diet—have never smoked much, nor have I ever been much of a drinker."

Helen Hayes is a very pretty lady. She was always pretty, a good example of beauty at every age she has passed through. A lifetime in the theater is downright hard work and shows in the faces of some actresses, but not in hers. Her skin is good, too, despite years of stage makeup. She's a combination of good living and a pleasant inner self. External beauty is not enough to last a lifetime; the inner self always eventually breaks through and makes the final statement. I remember being on the same television show a few years ago with Lillian Gish and seeing in her the same type of beauty Helen Hayes reflects; Lillian Gish was about eighty at the time.

The First Lady of the American theater was born in Washington, D. C., in 1900. She told me she began acting when she was five; her life on stage began at the age of seven in Broadway's *Old Dutch.*

Some of her great performances have been in *The Skin of Our Teeth, The Glass Menagerie, The Front Page,* and *Harvey.* And in the movies— *Farewell to Arms, Anastasia,* and others. *Victoria Regina* is the one that I will always remember. She's retired from the stage now and divides her time between Nyack, New York, and Mexico.

About ten years ago Ms. Hayes decided it was time to sell her lovely old Victorian home in Nyack. All her possessions were looked over and sorted for auction and she kept only the very personal ones. She left town after the sale of her house. But the sadness of giving up the house where she had lived with her husband, Charles MacArthur, and raised two children (son James and daughter Mary who died of polio in 1949) was too much. So, with joy, she bought back the house and returned to Nyack, much to the delight of the people in the area who hadn't been happy, either, about the prospect of the First Lady of Nyack leaving. She was part of them and they were accustomed to seeing her around town and taking her daily walk to and from Hook Mountain on the Hudson.

Just before that incident Helen Hayes had written a book called *A Gift of Joy,* an autobiographical work that is a joy to read because it differs from the usual celebrity autobiography. Through her personal vignettes, she shares a bit of the magic of life with her readers. After that she wrote *On Reflection* (1968) and *Twice Over Lightly* (1971) in collaboration with Anita Loos.

When Helen Hayes was a young girl she was not only very protected as she grew up, but she was also given many advantages. "I've taken just about every class in physical culture there was to be had." There were lessons with modern dancers Charles Weidman and Florence Fleming Noyes. There were lessons in breathing and diaphragm control from Frances Robinson Duff, the teacher of the famous singer Mary Garden. For footwork she worked with the sparring partner of the famous polo player Tommy Hitchcock.

All those opportunities to learn movement techniques add to the shaping of a person whether they are headed for the stage or any other type of life. Some people do grow up more advantaged than others, either due to wealth or parental educational level, but there is so much opportunity in this country for all young people that anyone interested in physical development can find low-cost and sometimes even free lessons in community recreation programs and through the schools. Helen Hayes was quite shielded from sickness and injury in her youth, but at the same time she did learn all types of body movement that helped her to grow up with good physical/emotional balance.

"I'm constantly stressing the importance of some kind of physical movement for young people in their formative years—whether it's the freedom for natural physical play in young childhood to sports participation, dancing, swimming, skating, or whatever takes the fancy. It's as important to future health as good nutrition.

"My body wants to be roly-poly, but my mind doesn't want it to be, so I have to keep an eye on that situation constantly because everything I eat goes right to my middle. Of course, at my age I suppose it doesn't matter very much whether or not I have a narrow waistline, but I do like to keep it as slim as I can anyway. It's a fight, though, because it's hereditary; my father was quite a roly-poly himself.

"So I always do my stretches. And then I do a special side-to-side stretch one hundred times very fast. A doctor prescribed it for me and I do it faithfully. I think it helps a little bit, but oh my, it's not much fun."

At the time I was talking to her she was on crutches to keep her weight off a very bad knee—a "Gerald Ford Knee" she said—and the subject of the knee sidetracked our exercise conversation, for it threatened to keep her from a pleasure trip to Florida if it became aggravated. I was curious about her use of the crutches, for she hadn't really learned to use them correctly, and was dragging them rather than using them as support—something her actor son, James, had also commented on during a visit the previous week. But she was clever enough to make up for it by not walking around too much.

Even with crutches she was able to show me the exercise that had been prescribed for her waistline. It's basically a good exercise, but she had been taught to do it rather like she was in Marine basic training. I explained to her that it was much more suitable for a man's body than hers, and not necessary to do one hundred times, and especially not so fast.

The male body needs quick, short-term muscle energy, and exercise by men is done accordingly; but the female body depends on long-term endurance, and is best served by exercise of that style.

I took the same exercise and instructed her to do it in slow motion so that she could get more of a stretch in each position, which would result in a feeling of refreshment rather than fatigue. I suggest the same for any other woman who battles the waistline spread.

Start in standing position. Bend to the side slowly with your arm stretching as far down the leg as possible. Pull chest up high and repeat to the other side, a minimum of eight times or as many more as you choose—a slow, exaggerated stretch coming away from the waistline.

Extend the exercise, while still in motion, by allowing the arms to join in the movement, windmill style as shown, for a greater waistline stretch.

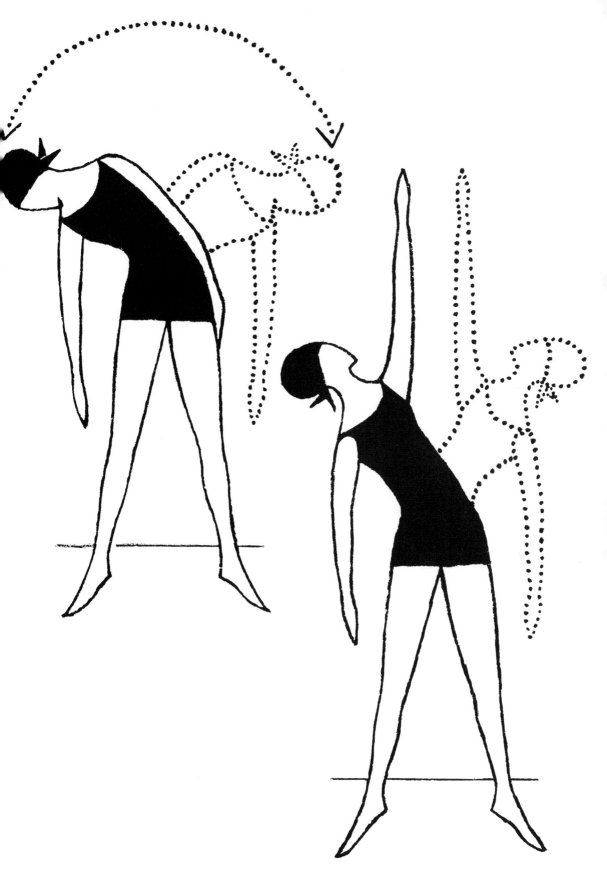

PETER SIMON

# Ruth Gordon

☼ *A veteran actress—*
*still going strong*

IN 1968 Ruth Gordon, at the age of seventy-one, won an Academy Award for best supporting actress in *Rosemary's Baby*. Other recent outstanding movies have been *Where's Poppa?* and *Harold and Maude*. As she says, she's the only actress whose "career peaked at seventy-five."

Generally we say that chronological age has nothing to do with how young or how old we are; it's how the person thinks and feels that's more important than making a point of the exact age. But in this case we're talking about a woman who seems to become more successful the older she gets, and her age therefore should be acclaimed.

Certainly she has enormous talent, and always has, and maybe she's been lucky in getting good roles that have been right for her these last few years. But if you look into the past of any successfully famous person you'll always see a lot of hard work that preceded any bit of luck. It's usually the person's special application of natural talent that creates such success.

Ruth Gordon was in the final stages of writing a second book when I interviewed her. She wrote *Myself Among Others* in 1971 and her new one is anticipated with great interest.

Ruth Gordon's unique and marvelous attitude toward life is reflected in her expressive face. She almost seems to see and know something that is beyond most of us. This quality is evident in all aspects of her work. She generates a special glow even in the way she walks.

Earlier in the book I mentioned that many, many celebrities are walkers, and the reasons they walk are varied. Ruth Gordon walks five miles a day. This daily walk is the clue to her outstanding success as an actress. She is the celebrity who walks to experience everything walking has to offer—satisfying, rhythmic exercise to fill the need of the body to move; relaxation or stimulation; detachment from life or involvement with it.

Maybe it's hard for most people to grasp the esoteric value of walking for exercise, but if you *can* imagine it and learn to apply it in your own life, I guarantee you will feel better, be happier, and experience more of what you want and are capable of. You must open your body to the world instead of closing it off from it, walk with perceptiveness and absorb what your senses receive.

You can change your physical concept of walking by changing your walking posture, making it easier to be perceptive along the way. The uptilt of the chin to raise the eye level, the resulting uplift of the diaphragm to permit better breathing, and the realigned spinal posture can make basic walking movement extremely beneficial to the body. Too simple for good exercise? No. The best solutions are the simple ones. Any woman who has led such a rich and fulfilling life as Ruth Gordon has is well worth emulating.

# Jan Peerce

✿ *The widely acclaimed opera singer*

W HEN you break an arm or a leg you experience a surprising sensation of weakness in that limb when the cast is removed. The weakness shouldn't really be a surprise because you know it's been totally immobilized during the period of mending. But it is, nevertheless, an unusual sensation not to be able to have total use of a limb once it is freed from a heavy cast.

One of my daughters broke a leg when she was nine months old and it was cast, mended and restored to full use within six weeks. Jan Peerce broke a leg past the age of sixty; regaining

full strength in his leg was more of a project. He feels very strongly about maintaining good health and is an exercising person anyway. Thus, he used exercise extensively as an aid in restoring the strength in his leg.

There were many exercises that he used—bending and stretching in various positions. The one most familiar to everyone is where you lie on your side, slowly lift up your leg, and then return it to its original position.

Jan Peerce is a tenor with great versatility. He sings bel canto (a style of singing characterized by brilliant vocal display and purity of tone); he sings Bach, Handel, and of course, opera. He has done Tevye in *Fiddler on the Roof,* and appeared in several movies including *Goodbye, Columbus,* directed by his son Larry. In addition to his concerts all over the world he can be seen on an occasional talk show and last year he gave seven master classes at Kent State University.

Before he acquired all this fame he experienced a long, hard climb from the Lower East Side of New York, made more difficult by the fact that his family was not sympathetic to his musical ambitions. After he married he made his living as a violinist and bandleader, and took voice lessons at night and on weekends. He then went from singing on the Borscht Circuit to Radio City Music Hall where he was heard on its Sunday afternoon broadcasts for many years. From there he went to the Metropolitan Opera and made his debut in *La Traviata* in the early forties. He has recently completed an autobiography.

Most of the exercising Jan Peerce does is of the bending, stretching type. But the exercise I found to be most interesting to pass on was marching in place. Running in place is something everybody's familiar with, but you don't often hear of someone exercising by marching in place.

"When you sit too long you lose your circulation," he said. "You keep the joints oiled by keeping them moving. That was my father's advice, and he lived to be ninety."

Some people might associate marching in place with regimented, militaristic movement. But try it sometime after you've been sitting awhile. Do it slowly, at least twenty times, lifting your knees high instead of marking time simply by shifting your weight from one foot to the other. You will be pleasantly surprised at the way it refreshes you.

It also serves your posture and physical poise with an action that pulls down the backs, tucks the buttocks under, draws in the abdominal muscles, and lifts the upper body. No wonder Jan Peerce always looks so straight!

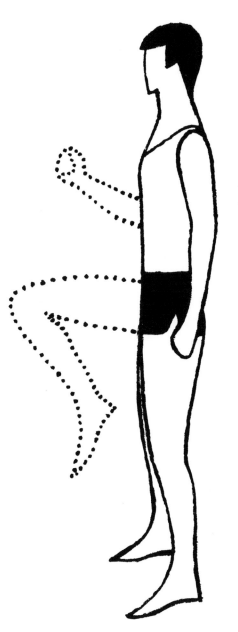

# Dr. and Mrs. Norman Vince Peale

*Religious leaders and best-selling inspirational writ*

THE OLDER the Peales get, the more they seem to do and accomplish—work, meet heavy speaking and travel commitments, but always return in time for church on Sundays. Dr. Norman Vincent Peale is the Minister of Marble Collegiate Church, Fifth Avenue, New York. In 1968 he officiated at the marriage of Julie Nixon and David Eisenhower.

He's also the author of nineteen books, including *The Power of Positive Thinking,* which has been enormously successful and has been translated into thirty-three languages. The title has even become almost a cliché in our language. His latest books include *You Can If You Think You Can* and *Norman Vincent Peale's Favorite Stories of Positive Faith.*

Ruth Stafford Peale is a career person, too. She evaluates her career as a three-part subject: wife, mother, writer, in that order. She has written numerous articles for such national magazines as *Reader's Digest, Woman's Day,* and *Coronet* and is the author of *The Adventures of Being a Wife.* She has also appeared on many national television programs.

Together the Peales publish the inspirational monthly magazine, *Guideposts,* an interfaith publication, which has a circulation of two and a half million. They have been married for forty-five years, and in 1964 a film was made about Dr. Peale's life titled *One Man's Way.*

On the subject of exercise they strongly believe that there is no real separation between the body and the mind in the total person. "The body and mind interact. Your physical being telescopes constantly to your mind," Ruth said. "One feeds and stimulates the other, and so you have a type of seesaw thing going on between body and mind with the life force as a middle balance point. One of the most valuable lessons life has to teach us is to find individual balance within ourselves and use it to develop ourselves as the people we are meant to be."

Walking and swimming are very important activities in the lives of Dr. and Mrs. Norman Vincent Peale. In detailing the actual appearance of their bodies, they say they both have waistlines with a tendency to spread. This would present a definite problem if they did not walk and swim as much as they do. They are also careful about their food intake, and try not to overeat.

The Peales take their summer vacations in the Swiss mountains so they can walk the trails. It bothers them that they only meet Europeans on the trails; the Americans are down below in the towns at the more traditional tourist spots, they say. They believe they should be up in the mountains enjoying the beautiful wild flowers and getting some exercise.

"Americans would discover a lot of beauty right here in our own country if they would get out and walk more," Dr. Peale said. "We have wild flowers and many, many beautiful things to see. Even in the cities you can walk and have a grand time looking at things as you get your exercise. I build up enthusiasm for life in general as I walk.

"The only trouble with walking in the city is that you have to stop for red lights and go up and down curbs, which breaks your stride," he added. "I like the feeling of the steadily paced momentum and relaxed thinking that you get with country walking."

But stopping for red lights and going up and down curbs has its advantages, too; when you stop for a light there's an automatic stomach muscle tightening that takes place as well as when you step down from the curb and climb up again on the other side. That's one of the many hidden values in walking for exercise.

You can simulate this "hidden exercise" as you walk through your home from one room to another. Walk four paces, pulling up to a sudden stop at an imaginery red light. Tighten the lower stomach muscles; hold until the "light turns green," release the muscles, step down the "curb," walk across the "street," and then step up, lifting your foot from the stomach area instead of using the knee. For extra exercise try to be conscious of using your entire body in any movement you do. Even in walking you do your body an injustice if you let the legs do all the work.

This simulated walking exercise is especially good for people who are over sixty and spend much of their time at home. It's good exercise you can do alone, at your own pace, in whatever you happen to be wearing.

The Peales have always valued exercise highly. Ruth will do as many as twenty or thirty laps in the pool at their country home, and her husband does almost as many. They exposed their three children (now grown with children of their own) to hiking, dancing, tennis, and other sports as they were growing up; their children have continued those activities and are now passing them on to their children —a part of child-raising that's just as important to hand down through the generations as manners, a respect for education, heirlooms, and other traditions.

Swimming is an excellent form of exercise for people over sixty (Norman is seventy-six), and it is also a specific way to keep your waistline in check. Study the illustrations of the Peales swimming the crawl stroke at the top of the next page. The entire body is involved in the movement from fingertips to toes; feet flutter kick and arms reach forward through the water, one at a time, and the waistline becomes smoothed out because of the muscle stretch action through the center of the body.

Everyone with access to a pool or body of water should take advantage and use that privilege for the sake of good general exercise movement and waistline control. There are community YMCA programs in many cities now that offer reasonable, reduced rates to senior citizens. If you don't know how to swim, it's never too late to learn.

Otherwise, you can join the league of pretenders and go swimming on top of your bed every day, duplicating the action of the crawl stroke, at least eight times. Safely supported by your bed, you can even go slower—since there is no danger of sinking—and exaggerate the stretching movement of the exercise so that you get a little extra benefit from your simulated swim. With an exercise like this simulated swim session you have complete control, for even though you are trying to extend your stroke to the maximum, there is no danger of muscle strain.

After your phony swim on top of your bed, "float" awhile, fully outstretched, totally relaxed, with a delightful feeling of bouyancy.

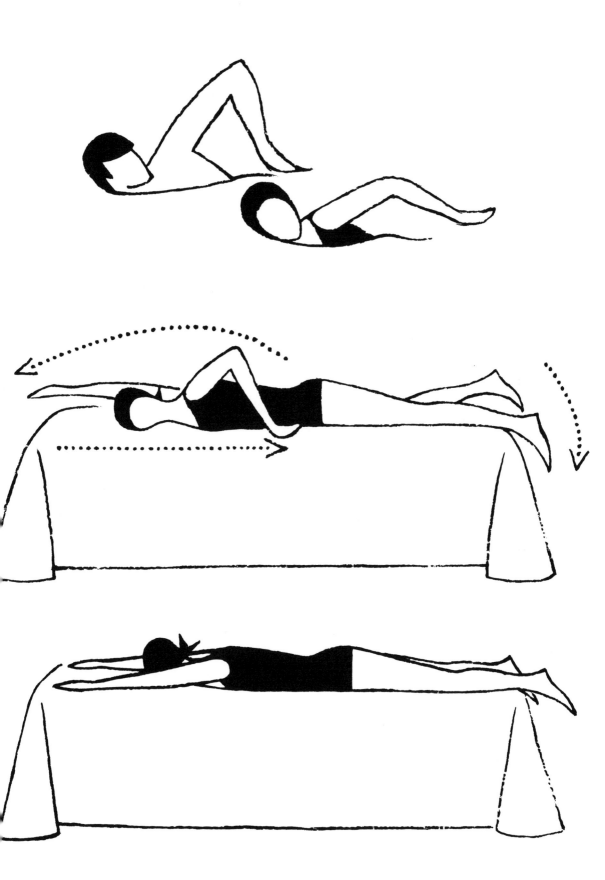

# SMALL BONED

HERE'S a chapter with an exercise range of almost zero to one hundred percent. Vivian Blaine exercises once in a while, Joyce Brothers exercises regularly, I do the dancer's warm-up every day, and Marjorie Holmes does more than all of us put together.

Celebrities exercise in a style that corresponds to their professional personality—complementary to it, to enhance it, or to express it. In an analysis of these women mentioned you can understand their exercise needs; when Vivian Blaine exercises it's to develop and extend herself for maximum audience projection; Joyce Brothers is an example of quiet, steady exercise used to promote good physical and emotional health; the exercise of Marjorie Holmes is an outward expression of her exuberance for life, and for me it is as basic and central as brushing my teeth.

As a short, small-boned person, where do you fit in? What exercise is right for you and serves both as an outlet for your energy and a developer of your physical/emotional personality?

Your body assumes the characteristics of the exercise style you practice. If you depend on jogging for daily exercise, your legs will begin to identify you as a runner. If you dance you will take on grace. If you learn Judo, T'ai Chi Ch'uan, or any of the martial arts, you develop an aura of body alertness, and so on. The best exercise for you as an individual is th style that brings out your personality When you fill that physical need you open up a whole new dimension to your life—a release. The most important thing to remember about exercise is that it must be your choice and your interest for it to be right for your body (with the exception of occasional therapeutic exercise prescribed to mend an injury or cure an illness).

Be very careful if you decide to tak an exercise class or follow television instruction; it is important to the boc to follow a teacher of the same sex a to exercise in the style of movement which you find comfortable. When y exercise under someone else's visual instruction, it's easy to think that you direct the movement of your own muscles and thus gain the individual advantage of the exercise. But that is not what happens.

What does happen is that you get a mental picture from his or her wor and movements, and then the reacti response takes place within your body in someone else's structural patterns instead of your own. If you are five feet tall and female, and the instructor is six feet tall and male, it is totally incongruous.

Just because a man was a former astronaut or pro athlete does not mean his body exercise is right for you. The implication that he is the epitome of fitness for everyone is foolish; he is the fitness example for people who want to become astronauts or pro athletes.

I think this is something that is grossly neglected in exercise endorsement and instruction. I saw a male exercise leader on daytime television instructing the "ladies at home" to do a body warm-up exercise like a boxer's movement—an alternating punch, two, three, four, and his commentary was "Oh, come on now, ladies, how can I help you if you don't really punch?" urging the women to accelerate and strengthen their arm thrusts. Now that particular muscle tension warm-up may be all right for his very developed male body, but has very little relevance for the ladies at home unless they are in training for the ring.

The short, small-boned woman has the body most vulnerable to such exercise misinstruction. Many short people would rather be tall, so to begin with there's a negative body attitude. When that same male instructor on television has the ladies at home marching around to cutesy organ music playing "Old MacDonald Had a Farm" as he calls cadence, they respond with conditioned parade-marching reflexes. When he shouts "Oh, that's wonderful!" the small lady physically overreacts to the childish conversation and meaningless exercise, and moves like a child, caricaturing her smallness when she really needs to be moving as an adult—developing her body to make the most of its delicate stature. Remember, it is just as attractive to be short and small boned as it is to be tall and large boned. The secret is in finding your best physical personality and developing it.

Examine more closely the very strong influence of words on your body. The most common advice in an exercise class is to "stand up straight and throw your shoulders back." This directive implies traits of moral integrity. Therefore, you subconsciously try to look like someone brave and strong and physically fit—obviously the leader of the class. If you are then directed to move around the room while the leader shouts out his reminders to keep your shoulders back, chest up, and so on, you automatically react accordingly, shaping your body to irrelevant and anatomically false patterns.

If you continue to follow exercise styles that do not complement your own body, you eventually shape and set your body to those alien styles. Physically, then, you are always behind the eight ball, never really achieving anything for your own body beyond general circulatory benefits.

Look around at people, bodies, activities, and movements. There are many models, many alternatives. What would you like your body to say about you? The following celebrities have all found their true physical expression. By following their examples, you can find yours!

# Vivian Blaine

✿ *A sparkling musical comedy star*

**V**IVIAN BLAINE was touring with the play *Light Up the Sky* when I talked to her about exercise. She was thoroughly enjoying the run but also looking forward to other interesting parts, which would be offered when the tour ended. I found it difficult to think of her as anyone other than Adelaide in *Guys and Dolls,* the role she made so famous in the fifties musical that keeps being done over and over by both amateur and professional theatrical groups.

She is a short, light, trim woman. "But I was very heavy at one time," she said. "At sixteen I weighed 150 pounds. At seventeen when I made my screen test I had dieted down to 116 by practically starving. My weight was a terrible problem at that time. I'd go on liquid diets and gain weight. I went from doctor to doctor with no results, until I finally found one who solved the problem."

The problem was water retention. She still has the problem, but once it was recognized she could control it with proper diet and medication. If you are a small-boned person like she is, carrying an excess amount of weight, regardless of light eating habits, I would suggest that you check with your doctor to determine if you have a water-retention problem. Once this problem is solved, you will look and feel better, too. You feel much more tired and sluggish when your body is retaining too much liquid.

And if you're inclined to short height and slight development, exercise is a much better way to create an illusion of height than wearing a high hair-style or unusually high heels and push up bras—all of which draw attention to and accentuate shortness because they're out of proportion to the body lines.

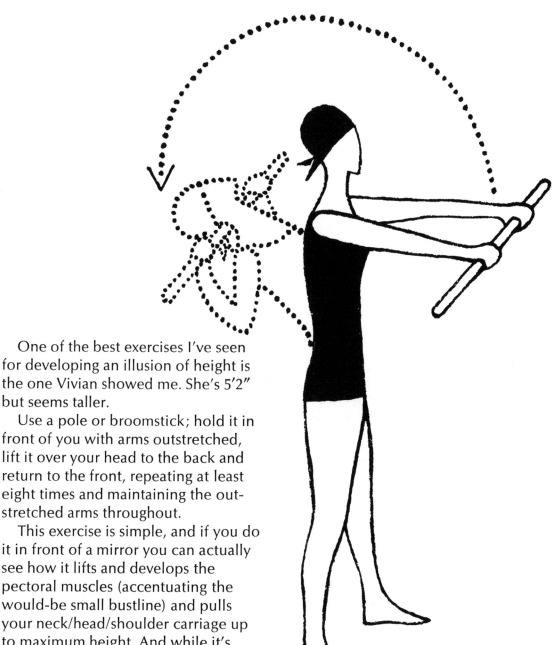

One of the best exercises I've seen for developing an illusion of height is the one Vivian showed me. She's 5'2" but seems taller.

Use a pole or broomstick; hold it in front of you with arms outstretched, lift it over your head to the back and return to the front, repeating at least eight times and maintaining the outstretched arms throughout.

This exercise is simple, and if you do it in front of a mirror you can actually see how it lifts and develops the pectoral muscles (accentuating the would-be small bustline) and pulls your neck/head/shoulder carriage up to maximum height. And while it's doing this, it's also forcing an uplifted pull throughout the entire body that is responsible for pulling in a protruding stomach and straightening your posture. The result really does create an illusion of being taller and more generously endowed, and it's also great for improving your posture.

# Marjorie Holmes

✿ The renowned inspirational
writer who has reached millions

Every morning she takes a hot and cold shower with the water coming on so strong that her skin is actually pummeled. After her shower she does a kind of rag doll shake—bending over completely loose and relaxed. This is followed by a floor touch, and then the familiar bicycle exercise, in which she concentrates on bringing each foot down slowly with control.

She goes into the kitchen, and while waiting for the coffee to perk does six or eight pliés using the stove counter as her ballet barre. She puts her leg up on the "barre" and bends forward to touch her knee—just as it's done in ballet class to stretch the muscles.

A plié is the base of the ballet dancer's movement. It begins every class as body warm-up movement and is used throughout the ballet in combination with other movements. It is a movement for developing a sense of balance—a bending of the knee (or knees)—a movement for making joints and muscles soft and pliable, and tendons flexible and elastic. The bending movement should be gradual and smooth. The legs must

"I LOVE my body. I'm very fond of my body and I don't intend to ever let it go!" Marjorie Holmes is a real body person. The fact that she weighs only one hundred pounds, is 4'10½" and in her early sixties, means nothing. Her capacity for living is enormous.

"Exercise is just as important as good nutrition. It gets to be a habit, and I just don't feel right without it," she told me.

out a short distance, treads water awhile, and then swims back. She does this before each meal three times a day, and sometimes at night she goes out for a skinny dip. (A skinny dip, by the way, is a swim *sans* suit and feels absolutely wonderful, especially in the dark!) The body is totally released to move with maximum freedom.

This is the Marjorie Holmes who wrote such bestsellers as *I've Got to Talk to Somebody, God; Love and Laughter; Who Am I, God; Nobody Else Will Listen; As Tall As My Heart; You and I and Yesterday; How Can I Find You, God; Two from Galilee;* and other religious, inspirational articles that appear regularly in magazines and newspapers. Her audience is wide, she is a source of inspiration, and many women have experienced help and great comfort from what she has written; she obviously strikes a chord that many women respond to.

*Two from Galilee* has recently been made into a movie and Marjorie has spent the last year working on the screenplay, in addition to keeping up her columns, articles, and other books in progress. Her energy reserve seems endless.

"Early in my career I had one short lucrative fling writing for the confession magazines. They were Sunday School stories compared to what is being published now, but I knew I was working for the wrong boss—on a dead-end street. One day a phrase from Dorothea Brande's book *Wake Up and Live* shook me: 'Are you working at failure?' The answer was so

be turned out from the hips, the knees open and over the toes, and the weight of the body evenly distributed on both feet, with the whole foot grasping the floor.

After Marjorie's kitchen pliés, that are shown above, she fixes her husband's breakfast, grabs her jump rope, and dashes outside for 125 skips —even in the rain and snow. And that's just her winter routine!

In the summer she swims three times a day at Lake Jackson in Manassas, Virginia, where she and her husband go for vacation. She keeps three bathing suits there so that one is dry all the time. In the morning before breakfast she puts one on, runs down the steps to the lake, dives in, swims loud and clear I turned down an assignment that would have meant a lot of money and never wrote another. It's as important to be proud of what you do with your talent as it is to be proud of your body. It's all one thing."

That's a very strong point that Marjorie made. It reflects her clear perspective and provides a key to the secret of her success and charisma. The pride in talent that each celebrity discovers at some point in his or her development is the quality that gives many the poise and security needed not only to go on but also to strive to be unique. It's something that everyone can learn but few seldom do, even though every person in this world is born with some form of talent or some personal characteristic that they can develop and of which they can be proud.

Her satisfaction with what she does overshadows her figure faults, which might be major problems to anyone else. As she says, "I'm a little sway-backed, and I wish my fanny didn't stick out, and I never had a very big bosom, but I don't care—I was still able to nurse all my babies!"

The small bosom is something I should elaborate on for the sake of all other women who are concerned with this problem. A clarification of facts will dispel many misconceived ideas.

The breasts are glands, not muscles; therefore it is not possible to increase them to a great extent. The various exercises that are recommended to increase the breasts actually work on the muscles underneath the breasts.

These muscles are developed to a point where they will hold the breasts higher and firmer and thus create the illusion of greater size.

The most realistic thing to do if you have small breasts is to continue the tension exercises you're probably already doing (extend elbows, and press and release fingertips together; this stimulates the muscles under breasts). Also, develop a highly held carriage to further create the illusion of a large bosom. Or, you can lift weights as Mae West is reputed to have done for years—and strengthen the underlying muscles even more. Keep an eye on the biceps so you don't overdevelop them in the process.

Or, you can remind yourself of a famous quote in history made by a man in reference to his small but lovely woman—". . . just the right size to fit the hand of a gentleman."

As an exercise "expert" I could have shown Marjorie some of the exercises that dancers do to counter swaybacks and fannies that stick out. But for one who is in such good physical shape (she even takes her jump rope in her suitcase when she travels) and is so satisfied, it just didn't seem important. Besides, she didn't even ask me.

But if you are swaybacked and your fanny sticks out and you're not happy about it, you can do the following exercise while you're standing at the stove preparing breakfast or lunch or dinner—or standing any place, for that matter. Stand in good posture, heels together, with feet turned out. Tighten the pelvic muscles and force them slightly forward as you tighten and tuck your buttocks under to a count of one. Hold for two and three; release on count four. Be sure to keep your good posture. Do this eight times and try to hang on to the position as long as you can after you've finished the exercise, with the idea of maintaining correct posture at all times. You want to strengthen your stomach muscles so they can help you teach your body to shift the weight displacement that causes the swayback and resulting buttock protrusion.

# Dr. Joyce Brothers

☼ *Television's top media psychologist*

that I used to try to hide myself. But then the rest of my body grew into proportion and it was all right." Her figure, by the way, is good—well proportioned and trim.

She has a swimming pool in the basement of her house and swims one to two miles a day. "The only problem is my hair. There just doesn't seem to be a bathing cap that adequately covers my hair and keeps it dry." I assured her there are worse problems —like not having a pool in your basement at all. (For the millions of us who do not, there is always the local Y, which is quite economical to join.)

Dr. Brothers is a firm believer in exercise. Because she is a psychologist I brought up the guilt feelings that people experience when they think they are not doing enough exercise—feelings that are destructive.

The unpublicized reasons so many people don't exercise is because they haven't found a form that doesn't bore them. Another reason is that many people still have the idea that if it feels good it must not be doing any good, because exercise is supposed to be disciplined physical effort. Actually, the reverse is true.

THE LADY who won $134,000 on the $64,000 Question and Challenge Show by knowing all the right answers on the subject of boxing and then went on to become a media psychologist was born in New York City, October 20, 1928, graduated from Cornell, and received her doctorate in psychology at Columbia.

She is only 5'1". "But my shortness never bothered me," she says. The only time my figure did give me anguish was in adolescence; suddenly I was all bosom, and was so embarrassed by it

For instance, stretching in bed in the mornings is one of the best things you can do for your body, because it safely uses your total muscle structure (if you stretch to maximum), and the breathing that automatically accompanies the stretching brings oxygen into your body cells and stimulates your circulation. But because so many people feel guilty about self-indulgence of this sort—stretching in bed does feel good—they pass up that pleasure and drag themselves out of bed without it. Dr. Brothers found this concept interesting.

The more personal exercise information she divulged forced me to have a measure of respect for bicycle machines. Dr. Brothers has one, and rides it while she watches television. The idea of hopping on your "bicycle" when you turn on the tube, and having the option to "ride away" if the show isn't any good, is enough to make that otherwise boring apparatus not so boring after all. "Ride" for at least ten minutes a day.

Just make sure you're riding correctly, whether it's on a real bicycle or a machine. Use the muscle action through your whole body as you pump the wheels instead of making your legs do all the work, spinning your wheels, and thus not receiving the full benefit of this exercise.

# Ann Smith

☼ *Writer, dancer, and exercise expert*

**W**HEN I was a child I was so little and skinny that the neighbors thought I didn't get enough to eat; my sisters and brothers were normal sizes, so obviously we did have enough food. I was just picky, preferring steaks and butter to stews and margarine. And I was sick all the time—asthma and all the childhood diseases, usually with complications.

In school I was always the smallest one in the class. When I entered high school I was 4'10"; when I graduated four years later I was 5'8½". Now, as I look back, I think it was just arrested development. However, I'm one of those rare people who spent the first fifteen years of life wishing to be tall, and had my wish granted. I am still a small-boned person, but a tall one, and each year I get healthier.

My childhood was spent in Western Springs, Illinois—a beautiful little Chicago suburban town that's great for raising children. (It's also known as the location of Billy Graham's first church.) Along with all other proper girls I was sent to college to join a sorority and find a husband, which I eventually did. I was an education major at Miami University in Oxford, Ohio. But boredom set in before my graduation or my marriage, and I left college to pursue a life that held greater interest for me.

All my life I danced. My mother was a dancer, a proponent of the early modern dance style. Although I always hated that "interpretive dance," I was her star pupil. I longed to study ballet, but the early disciples of modern dance were rebelling against the formality of this style. Because my mother didn't want to lose face, it wasn't until she eventually retired from teaching that it was all right for me to study ballet. Tap was permitted, however, and I became a nifty little tap dancer. I can still do a pretty quick shuffle-off-to-Buffalo.

After leaving college I concentrated on dance, working by day as a secretary/model at the Merchandise Mart in Chicago, studying dance every night, and modeling as a dancer for various artists on weekends. When I began to audition for dance companies, or shows, it always seemed I was too tall. I soon decided my life in dance would be better spent as a teacher instead of a performer, which worked out to be absolutely true because teaching suits my personality.

Dance has been the center of my life. The activity and discipline it provided helped me to have three children by natural childbirth. It also enabled me to have a satisfying career of teaching and writing. (I taught every day for twenty years, including the time during three pregnancies.)

When we were living in Milwaukee, Wisconsin, in order to make extra money, I began teaching adults the warm-up stretching of the dancer. This proved to me that the dancer's exercise regimen was a far more pleasant form of exercise than most; dancers have strong, healthy, proportionate bodies. My classes in stretch exercise grew immediately, and when we moved to New York two years later and I began teaching both modern dance and stretch exercise there, my classes grew to waiting-list proportions. Women responded to that style of exercise and stayed with it.

At that point I began writing articles about the subject. *Seventeen* magazine published the first one called "Do Exercises Work?" Then came other articles, radio and television appearances, and the publication of my book *Stretch,* a graceful, easy exercise system for women based on the exercises of the dancer.

I have become healthier over the years, and have my daily stretch exercising to thank for this. My ideas on exercise in general are evident throughout this book, but there are a few practical secrets I'd like to share with you.

We think of exercise as a way to keep healthy, to burn off calories, and to improve our figures. But exercise is also a great aid in relaxing and relieving tension, and that's a very important function. So I've pulled out of my repertoire an "instant relaxer" that anyone can use to relieve body tension. It can be done any time of the day. I've also included some other relaxing exercises and tension relievers, which can be performed after the "instant relaxer."

Lie on the floor and place your ankles on the edge of a chair. If your body is relaxed, your feet automatically fall apart; if not, they stay parallel to each other. If you let yourself go and unlock your body tension, you will see your feet fall apart. Stay in the relaxed position as long as you choose —at least five minutes.

The value in this "instant relaxer" is in the control you learn, allowing your body to unwind. Don't cheat by opening your feet. Relax and let them fall open naturally, by themselves.

Once you are relaxed you can extend your arms over your head on the floor, and then return them to your sides. This will make your torso a little more supple.

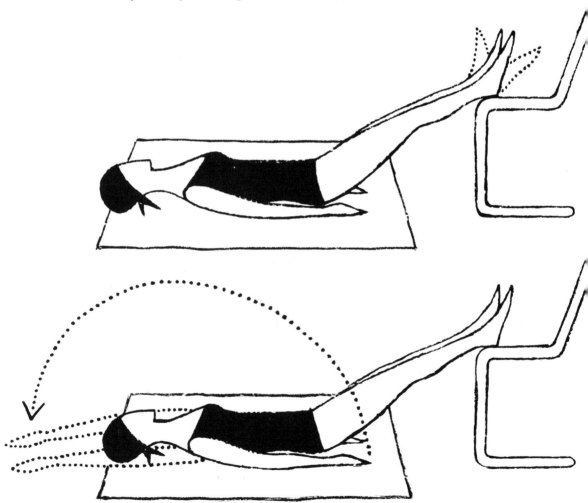

For further relaxing and unwinding, do the two exercises pictured here—first with feet together and then with feet spread. Reach slowly for the ceiling, one arm at a time, alternating arms four times.

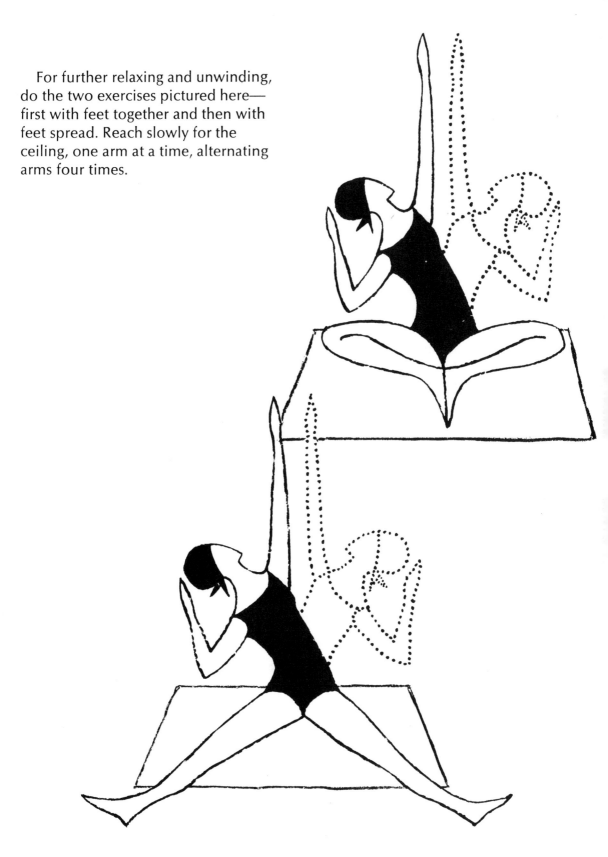

# LARGE BONED

CONSIDERING our physical evolution, we have had a lot to contend with. It has taken us millions of years of spinal change to reach our vertical posture. Animals are born with the same posture they will maintain throughout their lives, in movement and at rest. We must develop, from a fetal position, the ability to sit, crawl, stand, and become upright. At rest we change our skeletal positions from vertical to horizontal. For all that, we really do quite well; with exercise to maintain satisfactory strength, flexibility, and good posture, we do even better.

The large-boned person has the biggest maintenance job of all, because of the lengths and weights of the bones and the total structure of the skeleton. There is just that much more person to maneuver around.

Madeline McWhinney, President of the First Women's Bank in New York, is 5'10" and a large-boned woman. She is more lean than fat, and because she is proportionate and very active, she moves as easily as a short, small-boned woman. Sam Huff, a former pro football player, is trained and conditioned for movement, so he has no problem manipulating his frame.

But the body that is called the full figure does have greater problems of space, movement, speed, and agility to contend with. This is the body that depends on the charisma of the person to make it a body beautiful. It must move and blend gracefully, for it will undoubtedly stand out in a crowd.

If a full-figured person is a dull person, the body takes on a massively dumpy appearance. But if the person has an interesting mind and personality, like an Eleanor Roosevelt, the body is the person.

Eleanor Roosevelt held her head high and drew attention to her mind and personality. This gave her body a dignity, which would otherwise have been lacking.

When you see the regally developed charisma of the full-figured person you see poise, pride, and proper proportions. If the person so built lacks such body style, you see bad posture, dumpiness, and a general shapelessness that often reflects the person inside the body.

Looking over pictures of famous women in history (if you can go by pictures) you can find a few full-figured women with body personality —Queen Boudicca, the warrior Celtic queen who led the Britons' victory over the Romans; Eleanor of Aquitane, crusader, political prisoner, Queen of the Troubadours; Vittoria Colonna, Renaissance poetess; and Susan B. Anthony, pioneer of women's rights.

I make a point of naming these women because they, like Eleanor Roosevelt, show that when the mind, the talent, and the inner person is developed so, too, is the body. This is true of every body type, but in the large person it seems to be even more true.

In our contemporary scene, we also have full-figured people with body charisma. I have used Elinor Ross, an opera singer, and B. B. King, a blues singer, as examples in this chapter.

Because of hormonal differences between males and females, males develop larger, squarer bone structure across the shoulders and are more muscular than women. Therefore, men are able to lift and carry larger loads, and when exercising should move in larger, more flexed motions to maintain that structure and muscle strength.

Men also develop larger rib cages than women and have larger hands. Another anatomical difference between men and women is, of course, the pelvis; in the male it is narrow, heavy, compact; in the female it is broad, light, capacious.

Exercise style for the full-figured person should be chosen carefully; concentrated use of calisthenics would overdevelop the body to monsterlike style. But there are some recreational exercises that work very well.

Archery is good exercise because of the accent on the uplift posture—the regal bearing; fencing is good for agility; bowling develops coordination; canoeing develops balance; walking and running are good for the heart, for muscle endurance and balance; fly fishing and hiking aid heart action, muscle endurance, and muscle power; rowing does all that, plus helps coordination. The best pleasure exercise of all is swimming, because the whole body becomes involved.

Large-boned people like Sam Huff and Madeline McWhinney (President of the First Women's Bank) don't have to be as selective in choosing exercise for its style because they're not so inclined to carry the extra weight of the full-figured person. But there is vulnerability to back strain simply because the large-boned person usually has a long back.

Back strain can produce serious problems that are difficult to correct. Much of the time the problems can be traced to tension which creates misalignment of the body, and makes you more susceptible to injury.

Don't ever negate any exercise just because it might strain the back. There's a very simple way to determine whether an exercise is good or not good for your back or your particular body structure: if it hurts, don't do it— if it doesn't hurt, it's all right. Your body will tell you. Any organism that has adapted so well to its own evolution is reliable enough to put out valid signals; all you have to do is learn to interpret them.

# Elinor Ross

☼ *Metropolitan Opera's dramatic soprano*

"MOST opera singers are overweight according to the insurance charts," Elinor Ross told me. "But would you believe I'm one of the smallest of the dramatic sopranos? I'm five feet six inches, weigh about one hundred and sixty-five pounds, and wear a size sixteen."

Elinor joined the Metropolitan Opera during the 1969-70 season. She sings *Turandot* and *Cavalleria Rusticana,* and made her Italian debut in *La Forza del Destino.* In the fall of 1975 she sang *La Gioconda* for the first time at the Met, and is now working with the coach of the late Kirsten Flagstad, one of the great singers of the past, in preparation for singing the Wagnerian operas.

Most voices can be matched to various body structures, Elinor explained to me. Among the men, tenors are inclined to be short and barrel chested; baritones and basses are usually tall. Among the women, coloratura sopranos are usually petite with small voices like the great Lily Pons. Joan Sutherland and Beverly Sills, who are dramatic coloratura sopranos, are larger. The mezzo soprano and the dramatic sopranos are often larger women, who tend to have big faces, short necks, and broad chests like Elinor. The development of a fine singing voice is relative to the development of the proper body to house it.

"I was always a bit strange compared to the other children I grew up with. To begin with, I lived in Tampa, Florida, because my parents were native Floridians, which was unusual. We lived on the wrong side of town, I was a fat kid with a voice, and we weren't even Italian. You know, people used to think only Italians could sing. So I skipped grades, made the honor societies, and was out of school at fifteen and on to serious voice study.

"None of that 'not fitting in' ever bothered me too much, but I think it bothered my relatives. Now, of course, they're all very proud of me and glad I'm the way I am. Isn't it sad the way our society puts so much pressure on children to conform and then expects individual achievement as adults? You must be very strong to be able to protect and develop a talent."

There is a rich mellowness, a maturity to the voice of the dramatic soprano—far different from the technical virtuosity of the coloratura in which you hear the high, fast trills. "I will sacrifice technical singing any day for a beautiful sound," Elinor said. "It's a responsibility to my voice and to my audience to get the most beautiful sound I can from it."

She also told me that even though she's considered overweight on insurance charts, and is visibly a large woman with a full figure, she dares not go below 145 pounds. If she does she has no stamina, and her voice thins out. That doesn't mean she can ignore her weight and become as heavy as she chooses; on the contrary, she must be very careful to keep from gaining too much. At one time she had gained forty pounds, and though she was singing all right she knew it wasn't very good for her health. Elinor is a vital person who enjoys life and wants to live as long as possible.

Every once in a while one of the dancers from the Met goes to her apartment to help her exercise. She much prefers that to any gymnasium exercising—an example of how famous people instinctively know what's best for them; the full-figured woman does not belong in calisthenic exercise programs because the possibility of overdevelopment from flexion exercise is very strong. Doing the more feminine dancers' stretch exercise is much more suitable for her. She also walks, rides a bicycle, and plays tennis occasionally.

Speaking of instinct, the subject of sex as exercise came up for discussion. It's good exercise. Experts have been analyzing the exercise value in sexual activity and have found that fulfilling sexual need can remove some of the desire to eat. The sex response is believed to be in the same area of the brain as appetite control. Therefore, one affects the other. Because of increased energy expenditure, 200 calories can also be burned off during sexual intercourse—a cumulative weight loss of five pounds per month.

The dancers from the Met have Elinor do the same body warm-up stretching that they themselves do every day—a variety of slow muscle stretching movements that work the entire body, stimulate, strengthen, and proportion it. In the process, calories do, of course, get burned off, but that's rather incidental to the more visual benefit of a firm, attractive figure.

The first exercise shown is a ballet exercise that stretches the inner thigh muscles. It's especially good in helping a large woman prevent heavy, loose thighs. With hands on ankles, press down with the force of the elbows eight times, gently but firmly.

In the next exercises, which are done in the more openly extended stretch of the modern dance style, stand in good posture with feet apart; reach straight down to the side as far as you can four times, making sure the hand goes straight down the side of the leg to maintain proper body alignment.

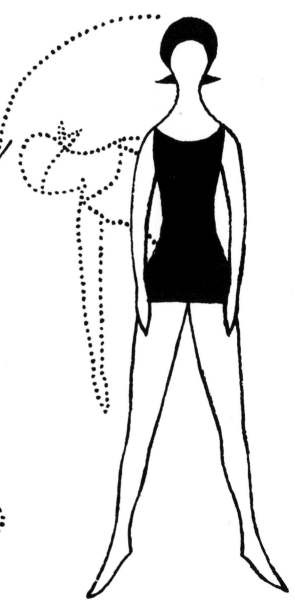

Return to upright position. Repeat on other side. Do this twice on each side, slowly. Do not jerk. You should feel a very definite body-stretching sensation on the side of your torso if you are reaching to the maximum. This is a good stretch and means that you are working off extra fat along the side and tightening the muscle tone.

Then enlarge the movement area by reaching down, out to the side, up and return to starting position, alternating sides four times. Do it smoothly, without jerking, and strive for a maximum reach at all points.

# Madeline McWhinney

☼ *President of the First Women's Bank*

MADELINE McWHINNEY is the President of The First Women's Bank in New York—the first commercial bank in the United States to be non-discriminatory in its hiring, promotion, and credit policies. It is making a special effort to serve women in a wide variety of services, including the granting of loans without requiring the signature of a husband or father as co-signer, instruction on financial matters, and, of course, the usual checking and savings accounts.

Before her presidency, Madeline was Assistant Vice-President of the Federal Reserve Bank of New York—the first woman officer—and she has an impressive list of accomplishments that began when she graduated magna cum laude in 1943 from Smith College. Both Smith and New York University, where she received an MBA in finance with highest academic standing, have awarded her their highest tributes for outstanding career success and for contributions to the community. She is married to Dr. John D. Dale, President of Dale Elliott Co., Management Consultants, and is the mother of a twelve-year-old son.

This financial expert is 5'10"—a woman with large bones. She is active, her bone structure is well-proportioned, and the only figure problem that she and many tall women have is buying clothes. It is difficult for a tall, large-boned woman to find good quality, attractively styled clothes that fit well—especially shoes, size eleven. "Most of what's available is cheaply made and not in line with present styling."

Madeline walks because it's the most dependable way to get any place. She also runs as much as she walks, because it's the quickest way to get some place —up and down stairs, to make appointments, and to save time. "I never have time for any other exercise," she said, "but if I did have the time I would also play tennis."

Like every other woman who's just given birth, she was told to exercise to firm up her stomach muscles after her son was born. Somehow she never could find the time to do the prescribed exercises, so she finally just resigned herself to the fact that she'd never have a perfectly flat stomach. (Not many people do, but one thing that helps after childbirth is to alternately tighten and relax the stomach muscles every time you're lying in bed on your back. It forces a return of the stomach muscle tone.)

"I've discovered that picking up sticks in the back yard is better than fifty-two push-ups anyway."

Madeline McWhinney is healthy and well-proportioned, so don't ever underestimate the exercise value of picking up sticks in the back yard, or picking up anything any place. Simulate this exercise four times a day: after bending over, inhale and rise by using your stomach muscles, and let your backbone return to its upright position one vertebrae at a time.

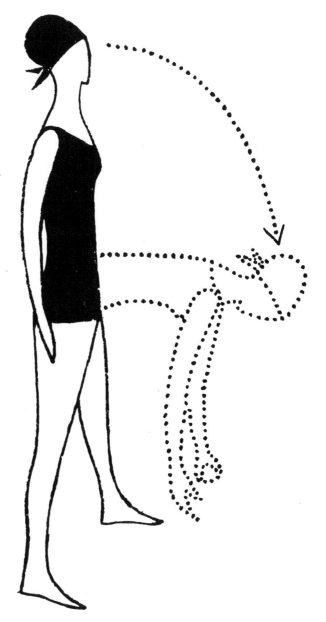

# B. B. King

☼ *The ever-popular
blues/rock singer*

He WAS born Riley B. King, September 16, 1925, on a Mississippi Delta cotton plantation near Indianola, Mississippi. He sang in church choirs as a child and started playing the guitar at age nine. In the Army during World War II he began singing the blues, and in 1948, while working at WDIA, Memphis radio, he acquired the name of B. B. King.

In the late sixties he found himself in demand before young white audiences who were eager to hear authentic blues. These audiences had been raised on heavily blues-influenced rock. Today he is recognized as one of the most popular blues musicians.

B. B. King is an unpretentious performer who establishes an intimate rapport with his listeners by being himself, performing as he really is. He is a quiet person, inclined to be shy; therefore, appearing before large audiences does not come easily to him.

For that reason he walks before concerts. He finds it calms him and steadies his nerves. Walking is easier and quieter at night, by the way, than it is in the daytime. That's because there is little visual distraction, and the body can move in a simple, basic pattern, unself-consciously.

Walking is B. B. King's exercise, but for him it is more then exercise; it is physical movement that complements his total personality. It relieves his tension and makes it possible for him to project and share the beauty of the blues with his audience in a natural way.

Many performers walk for exercise. It fills a very definite body need—a steady, rhythmic pattern of body movement that keeps the total body in tune without jarring it. During a performance a good artist gives so totally of himself that he needs some way to keep his physical/emotional person stabilized; for B. B. King it is walking.

He became a "walker" early in his life, walking ten miles daily to attend a one-room schoolhouse with eighty-six students and one teacher. When such a pattern is started as a child on a regular basis, it is quite natural to continue it as an adult. Walking, as an exercise form, is quite natural for anyone to take up, just as easily as B. B. King or any other performer has done.

There's a good exercise B. B. King could also do in the morning after a performance to maintain his body tone. It's in keeping with the shape of his round, large-boned body and complementary to his personality.

Stand in good posture with feet apart; stretch one arm toward the ceiling and the other toward the floor; hold, and reverse to the other side. Repeat this slowly four times, looking at the ceiling with each stretch. Then repeat it four more times, looking at the floor with each stretch.

# Sam Huff

FOOTBALL players are usually large-boned men; it isn't necessarily true that they are also exceptionally tall, although Sam Huff is 6'1" and anything over six feet is considered tall to most people. Sam is one of the NFL's all-time linebackers who's played for both the Redskins and the New York Giants. He now broadcasts the Redskins' games for WMAL radio in Washington. Athletes and dancers get into the habit of constant conditioning and body care. "When I left the game five years ago I was determined not to let myself go," Sam said. When a dancer stops performing she doesn't let herself go either, because movement for them both is habitual.

Sam weighed 230 when he stopped playing. This weight was all right for pro football when he needed it, but too much for regular living, so he dieted for a month and settled at 210. He feels this is a good weight for him to maintain. Most men his height would be more healthy and comfortable at about 185, but his bone structure needs the heavier muscle protection, especially in his upper body and torso.

"My biggest problem is too much stomach. Sonny Jurgensen and I have always had to work on that. He and I would have to exercise twice as hard as anyone else."

To control his stomach he does sit-ups, which are right for him. To keep in shape generally he lifts weights about three nights a week, plays golf, and walks a lot. He has had a sauna built in his home and uses that regularly.

Home is in Alexandria, Virginia, where he lives with his wife and three children; the youngest, age sixteen, plays football at Ft. Hunt High School.

Sam came from Farmington, West Virginia, where his father was a coal miner. The family was rather poor, and he was one of six children. He considered himself fortunate in receiving an athletic scholarship to West Virginia University; after that he went on to pro football. His life and career have been covered on television, in *Time* magazine, and many other publications from time to time.

Now he's Director, Market Development for Marriott Hotels, Inc. In this phase of his career he's been involved in the development of exercise clubs in many of the hotels—a worthwhile addition these days since the American businessman has become much more conscious of the danger of high cholesterol and the need to exercise frequently.

Many physicians now believe that a high cholesterol level in the blood is not the direct cause of coronary artery disease unless the level of another blood fat, triglyceride, is also elevated. Some of the recent findings in exercise research have shown that one total body exercise session will reduce the triglyceride level in the body and keep it down for three days. It's the triglycerides that trigger the fatty acids that make the cholesterol count dangerous and cause heart attacks. This is probably the greatest argument for exercise there is, for it means that if you exercise your entire body vigorously (in whatever style you choose) every two and a half days, you can control the triglyceride level and reduce your vulnerability to coronary artery disease.

Until women reach the menopausal years they do not have to be quite as concerned with the dangers of high cholesterol in their system because they are protected by estrogen, a hormone men don't have.

"Exercise to me is not fun. I think the best way to get it is with a group," Sam said. "In an exercise club at least you can practice self-discipline together. That's one of the things I miss about playing football—not the exercising as such—but the team spirit, the physically satisfying effort of working together and making something happen."

In the picture that follows, Sam demonstrates one of the various exercise machines in the Chicago Marriott Hotel. Machines can't provide the same human pleasure you get from recreational exercise but they can relieve the fatigue and strain of the traveling business person while away from home and help maintain physical health.

Since Sam Huff left the game, more and more of the amateur and pro teams have been turning to the dancers' regimen for exercise. Some teams have even used dancers to train them in this style. The UCLA track team was one of the earliest. The Los Angeles Rams have adopted a whole set of stretch exercises as part of their regular training. They use them at the beginning of their hard workouts to warm up the body and develop greater flexibility. They also use the dancers' exercise at the end of their workouts, because it takes the lactic acid out of the system and cools the players down so they don't get any pulls—similar to the way racehorses are handled after a race.

(Muscles are built up from amino acids, which are derived from protein foods. They are fueled by fats and a starch called glycogen. During strenuous body use, such as occurs in football playing, not enough oxygen may be available for the complete combustion of the fats and glycogen, so lactic acid forms in the muscles and causes extreme fatigue.)

Athletes have found that stretch exercising provides them with more flexible strength and endurance, and better maneuverability. They also experience fewer hamstring pulls and other serious muscle injuries that could keep them out of the game.

One very effective exercise the Los Angeles Rams use, which would also

CHICAGO PHOTOGRAPHERS

help Sam Huff keep his stomach flat, is shown below. With a partner, sit facing each other on the floor. Hold hands, spread legs, and interlock feet. One person leans back as far as possible as the other leans forward; then they reverse and continue the motion, pulling up each time as in a regular sit-up. Working with a partner with the legs spread provides much greater benefit to the stomach muscle tone. If the partners are of unequal height the position should be adjusted by holding wrists and interlocking feet at a higher leg point. Find the position in which you can work together without strain.

Dance teachers will frequently introduce this partner stretch to their young classes as a novelty. High school physical education teachers find teenagers enjoy this exercise. I like it better than the regular solo sit-up because it accomplishes more with less strain. If in the beginning you notice too much uncomfortable muscle pull in the upper inner legs, adjust the position with your partner by narrowing the leg spread, and move back from each other. Understand that the muscles in those upper inner legs do not get used often and they are inclined to be a bit tight. Repeat exercise four times.

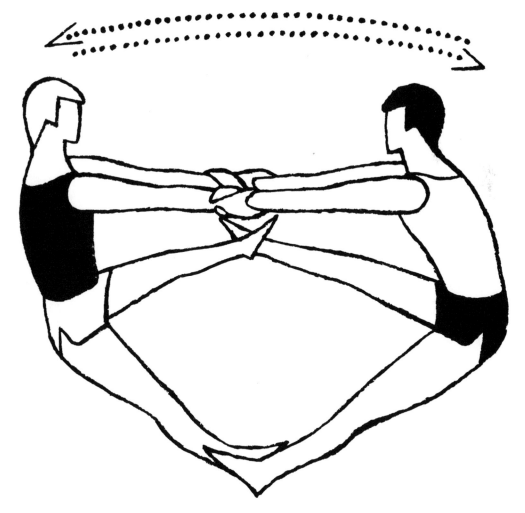

# WEIGHT PROBLEMS

BODY weight is determined by what food and how much of it goes into the mouth; how fast or how slowly the individual body chemistry uses it and converts it into "fuel"; and then how much exercise is done to use it. Some people can eat enormous amounts of food and not gain a pound; the opposite is true of others.

Problems of weight are usually associated with the overweight, but there are people who are underweight who have problems, too. The Amazing Kreskin, the mentalist, has a very fast metabolism and uses up his food so rapidly that he must eat five meals a day. Walking and hiking seem to provide enough exercise for him.

Ideally, the thin person could have an exercise program of two extremes. The first part would be a stylized form of movement—T'ai Chi Ch'uan, fencing, or anything that complements their positive body characteristics of lightness and agility. T'ai Chi Ch'uan is an especially good movement form for the thin person who is inclined to be high strung and nervous, because it is soft movement that has connected patterns and develops a harmony of body and mind.

The second part of a thin person's exercise program would employ a muscle-building form of exercise like isometrics. The purpose of isometrics is to work and develop muscles by pushing or pulling against an immovable object such as a wall, or by pitting the muscle against the opposition of another muscle. It's the "overload" principle of exercise physiology—that a muscle required to perform work beyond the usual intensity will grow strength. And research has shown that one hard, six- to eight-minute isometric contraction per workout can, over a period of six months, significantly increase the strength in a muscle.

There are more overweight people than underweight, however, and the big problem for them is how to get rid of excess fat and pounds. There are three safe methods that must be used in combination—food control, diet adjustment, and exercise. The aim is find the right balance of energy intake (food) and energy output (physical activity) for effective weight control. When the calories consumed in food equal those used to meet the body's needs, weight will remain about the same. When you eat more than this amount you will put on fat unless physical activity is increased proportionately. This is true for all ages and for both sexes.

Forty percent of a man's body weight is muscle. In women muscle amounts to only twenty-three percent. In place of the muscle weight, women have more hypodermal fatty tissue, their source of energy for long-term use. (Women are actually born with greater natural stamina than men, and in sports are less likely to be injured, because women do not generate as much fast, heavy momentum as men. The male body is constructed for short-term large amounts of energy expenditure; the female body is constructed for smaller amounts of muscle use over a long period of time.)

People watching their weight tend to concentrate on counting calories and forget the importance of exercise. When they do go on an exercise program, they are sometimes discouraged to learn after a few weeks that they look and feel better but have also gained a few pounds; this is because they are turning useless fat into muscle tone, and muscle weighs more than fat. In time it will find its balance.

Modest eating is body education that every man, woman, and child should learn, because most people eat more than they actually need. There is a difference between appetite and actual hunger. Appetite is a sensation based on the previous experience of eating foods that are pleasant to the taste, and the memory of the experience is a pleasant one. Hunger is the desire to eat based on the need felt by the body

when it has not had food for some time. Unfortunately, people tend to confuse the two words, especially those who overeat.

Craig Claiborne, the famous cook/writer, says you can get fatter from eating bad food than you can from eating good food. This is true. If you don't trust your taste buds enough to be able to discriminate between good and bad food, think of bad food as overstarched, overgreased, and oversugared. Anything you cut down on in that food area will benefit your body.

The food you eat supplies your energy. Energy use is divided between conscious and unconscious muscle use. Muscles that perform your conscious acts move you, make it possible for you to grasp and manipulate, balance yourself, breathe, swallow, eat, talk, and even breathe. Muscles that carry on your unconscious processes move your food through the digestive tract, pump blood through vessels, and expel your body waste. Proper food and exercise are necessary for good health.

It's not a good idea to exercise after you eat. The stomach requires a large blood supply to digest food, and exercise diverts the blood from the stomach to other muscles. The stomach's attempts to digest the food on less blood than it needs may cause discomfort. It's not good to exercise right before eating either. The body should have a chance to unwind before any intake of food.

Everybody needs a well-balanced diet and exercise. Here's how some celebrities who have weight problems have learned individual control.

# The Amazing Kreskin

☼ *Our most convincing ment*

THE Amazing Kreskin is a man who reads at the staggering rate of 7,000 words per minute, eats five full meals a day without gaining weight, and performs feats of thought perception, telepathy, precognition, and heightened recall that baffle and amaze people all over the world.

According to Kreskin, most people could be "amazing" if they would only try. His interest in becoming a mentalist started when he was a child, and after thirty years of developing his powers he has become well known for his feats of mental concentration.

Few people realize that such mental concentration speeds the rate at which the body burns off its calories. Kreskin is a thin person, and when he says that most people could also do amazing things with their minds if they'd try, can't help but think that overweight people especially should try becomi mentalists. According to Kreskin he sometimes loses two pounds during show!

When I am in a period of hard wo and intense concentration, I too beg to lose weight and can eat five meal; day without gaining an ounce. So I c understand how Kreskin's mental energy affects his metabolism. We discussed the possibility of teaching heavy people how to trigger this san burn-off that we both experience, b since neither of us are physicians we not qualified to go past a point of conjecture.

In the late thirties when he was five years old, Kreskin became influenced by the comic strip "Mandrake the Magician." It was Mandrake, he said, who prompted him to learn card and other traditional magic tricks and stimulated his interest in ESP. As early as eight he began "fooling around" with ESP, when he thought it would be a good trick to be able to pick up the thoughts—instead of the spoken words—of his playmates in the game "Hot and Cold." (In the game, an object is hidden from one of the players and the others direct him to it by saying "hot" or "cold.") Kreskin practiced on his younger brother for over three months before getting encouraging results.

It was from this childhood game that his "check test" feat emerged. In this act he invites anyone to hide the fee for his performance, and if he can't find it through ESP he forfeits payment. He claims he has forfeited a fee on only one occasion, when he was suffering from an eye injury and could not concentrate.

According to *The New York Times,* Kreskin was probably the youngest performing hypnotist in the world. He was performing half-hour shows around the country as a traveling magician when he was nine, and at eleven, was using hypnosis in his programs. By the time he was ten he had read all the books in the entire psychology department in the adult branch of his home town library in West Caldwell, New Jersey.

At Seton Hall University in South Orange, Kreskin earned an AB degree in Psychology. It was during college that he took the name Kreskin, which is a combination of his name and parts of the names of two magicians he respected—Keller and Houdini. Kreskin is now his stage name as well as his legal name. It had been George Kresge.

Exercise to Kreskin has a different

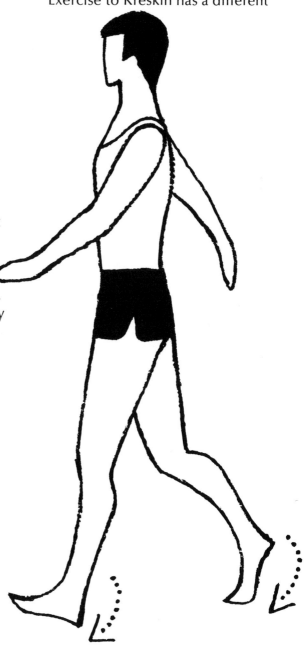

meaning than to most people. Yet, exercise is of great importance to him. He walks because it clears his mind and prepares him for his appearances before the public. Before every show he takes a one-mile walk to detach himself from the distracting things around him and build up an attitude of deep introspection. In a way, he psyches himself up to a totally positive frame of mind so that he can successfully harness the mental telepathy he demonstrates with an audience.

Walking is easier than standing still; the process of losing one's balance and quickly recovering it causes less strain if one is in motion rather than in a standing position. This is why people pace the floor instead of standing motionless in periods of stress. Walking movements are rhythmic and are good for our muscles, which require alternate activity and rest. In walking you actually roll forward from heel to toe alternately, in a natural rhythmic pendulum effect starting from the hip sockets—a very soothing body motion. But one side always tends to outwalk the other side (usually the same side as you write), so if a person were blindfolded he couldn't walk in a straight line—not even the Amazing Kreskin!

There are fifty-two little bones in the feet. It's quite easy to take the feet for granted, but they do, after all, make it possible for us to move from one place to another. They should make

contact with the ground, bearing an equally placed weight distribution between the heels and balls of the feet. If the body weight is allowed to pitch toward the arches, it can throw the entire body skeleton out of alignment —not to mention the weakening strain put on the arches themselves. Learn to use your feet properly, both in walking and standing. Get used to feeling the forward roll from heel to toe in the pendulum swing from the hips so you can release any hip tension and enjoy the rhythmic effect.

Bicycle riding would also be good exercise for Kreskin, and anyone else who's inclined to be thin and hyperactive. The legs begin the mechanical locomotion, and the trunk and arms

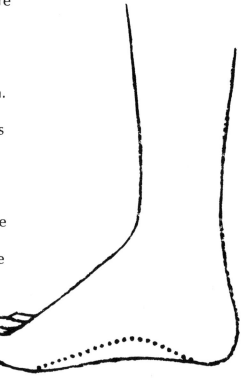

become involved in moving and controlling the bicycle. This involvement is muscular teamwork operating on a unifying line through the whole body. It's as though your feet are walking on the pedals.

The power from the muscles of your thighs and lower trunk move you and the bicycle forward. When one foot is up the other is down, and so each leg becomes alternately active and passive as the body moves forward.

You then have horizontal movement as a result of vertical effort, and you and the bicycle become one, moving together with alternate activity and rest. This results in an even healthier inhalation and exhalation process than you get from walking.

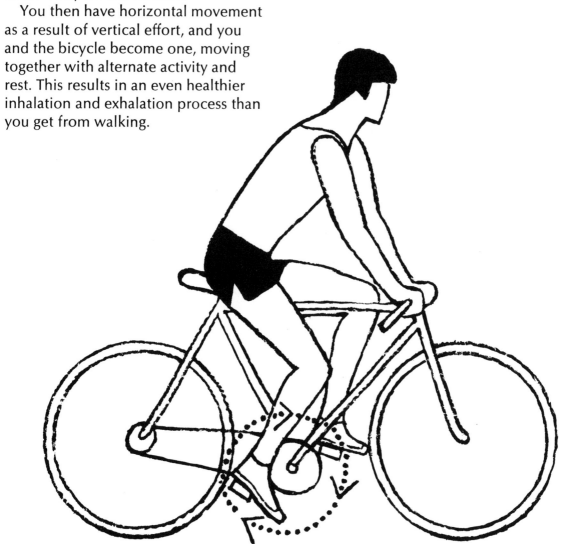

# Rubye Graham

☼ Seventeen *magazine's*
*executive editor*

IN 1974 Rubye Graham became the Executive Editor of *Seventeen* magazine. For fourteen years she had been fashion and beauty editor of the *Philadelphia Inquirer,* writing more than five thousand stories for the paper, many of them cabled from showings in Paris, Rome, and other international centers.

*Seventeen* magazine has undergone a transformation since Rubye became its executive editor. It has become streamlined as a result of reducing its page size. Ever since the debut of the magazine's smaller page size, Rubye has been aiming at a personal trans-formation, too; she feels herself in need of streamlining.

"I have always had pressure jobs," she said. "For me, pressure in the executive suite adds weight, because I react to pressure by eating. Numerous necessary business lunches also add to the problem. When I was twenty, I weighed one hundred and seven pounds. Each decade has added at least ten pounds to my frame. I have an average-type body and am well proportioned, but weight is my problem."

Rubye is dieting to lose twenty pounds. She doesn't believe in crash diets, but feels quite comfortable with basic high protein fare, a diet suggested by her doctor. When she diets, she also puts into effect an evenly paced exercise plan. The beauty editor at *Seventeen* suggested that she do some stretching exercises. Rubye, who often wears a leotard at home, says these stretch exercises make her feel very good.

I suggested swimming or tennis, too. A physical sport is excellent for burning off extra calories and syphoning off a lot of nervous energy. It also shapes up the body.

Rubye agreed with me, but said she really couldn't manage physical sport because she'd never had any conditioning. She grew up in a small Kentucky town, which had no facilities for tennis, gym, or swimming —even in the schools—and this was compounded by the fact that she had rheumatic fever when she was ten.

"This is a part of my youth that I regret very much—absolutely no body conditioning. I believe if you don't learn to use your body as a child, it becomes almost·impossible to learn as an adult. I've taken swimming and tennis lessons several times recently without any success at all—the coordination and reflexes just aren't there."

As a result of the lack of active sports participation in her childhod— no body-building at all—her body does not "feel" movement, even when she dances.

"As a result of what I missed in my teen years, I'm very aware of the importance of sports participation for our readers. That's why you'll find increased emphasis in the magazine on sports. We've had two sports figures— Olga Korbut and Chris Evert—on recent covers.

"I totally believe in the healthy, open sporting activity type of exercise like swimming, tennis, biking, jogging, and gymnastics," she continued. "These activities, combined with a sensible, nutritious diet, will develop healthy, strong, well-coordinated bodies."

Under Rubye's guidance, *Seventeen* magazine is leaning more and more toward the natural, realistic, and sports-oriented type of exercise. She finds their readers much prefer that to the traditional touch-your-toes-fifty-times shape-up exercises, which don't appeal to most people. She does think there are some girls who need shape-up exercises to take care of certain spots, but for a general exercise program, there's nothing that beats an exercise plan built around one or more sports.

I heartily approve of the magazine's editorial endorsement of the more natural, realistic ways for young women to exercise. It's about time.

Since Rubye does not participate in sports, her major form of exercise is walking, which she enjoys. She walks briskly, and that compensates somewhat for the other exercises she doesn't get.

Rubye's figure will always need her careful attention. But half the battle is recognizing the problem, understanding it, and working around it. And that she does.

Many women have grown up without enough natural body movement or participation in sports programs. Bonnie Prudden, an early advocate of physical fitness for both boys and girls, made the government aware of the inequity of physical education programs in our schools many years ago. However, action was not taken for a long time. She repeatedly made the point that we expect our girls to grow up and give birth to fine, healthy babies without properly conditioning their bodies.

The schools weren't the only ones at fault though; families and communities were likely to think of little girls as delicate creatures who needed protection instead of body workouts.

The physical future now looks better for girls, but for those of you who were born too early to benefit and suffer from Rubye's problems, here is the stretch exercise that I recommended for her, and one which was approved by her beauty editor. It complements her softly rounded appearance and personality, and it is within her physical capability. Over a period of time, it will evenly tighten her muscles and give her a smoothed-out appearance.

Rubye does it each morning after getting out of bed, in her office before lunch, at home before dinner, and at night before retiring. Because it is a total body stretch, she does it very smoothly and slowly, making sure that she is stretching away from her body the farthest areas she can reach. She also continues her brisk walking habit and, in combination with her dieting, is well on the way to the body that becomes her.

Stand with feet placed widely apart. With right arm reach forward from the waist, over to the left side, to the back and around to the right side—a smooth

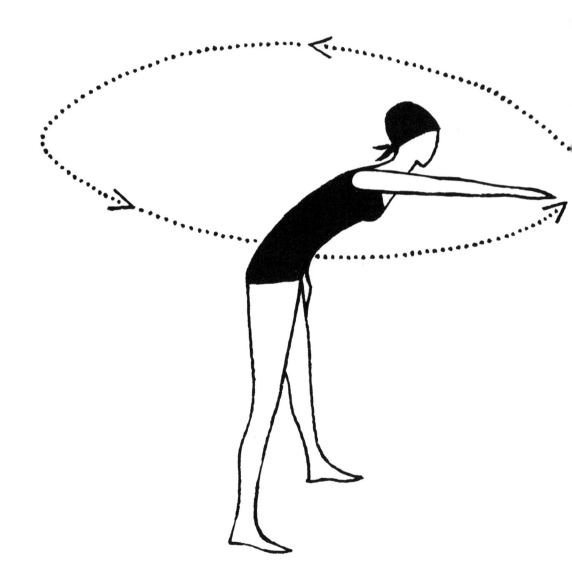

circular motion in which you are striving for a maximum reach during the entire circle. It is done four times around each side, very slowly.

If you're not used to the exercise it is possible that you'll get a little dizzy doing this, because when you reach to the back part of the circle, your equilibrium is upset. Keep your eyes focused on your hand as it goes around the body so you won't get dizzy.

For those who still experience some dizziness as you reach to the back, alter the movement by reaching straight up, as shown in the second drawing. You will still benefit from the exercise. If you do the exercise regularly, you will find that you can gradually work toward a steady back reach as your muscle tone becomes more secure and your equilibrium stabilized.

# Art Buchwald

✿ *The Capital's leading
syndicated humorist*

ONE OF the funniest and most
popular men in the newspaper world
is Art Buchwald. His columns on
political satire for the *Los Angeles
Times* syndicate appear in over five
hundred newspapers. He is also the
author of twenty books that display
the same type of humor as his newspaper columns.

In 1957 Art Buchwald became the
subject of newspaper headlines when
the White House Press Secretary, James
C. Hagerty, attacked one of his columns
as "unadulterated rot." President
Dwight D. Eisenhower was attending

a North Atlantic Treaty Organization
Conference in Paris at the time, and
while attending the press briefings
conducted by Hagerty, Art was struck
by the detailed coverage that news-
papermen gave to the President's
routine activities. In the column that
created the furor, Art satirized the
briefings by asking such questions as:
"What time did the President start
eating his grapefruit, Jim?" and, "Jim,
did the President speak to anyone before retiring?"

At a later news conference, Hagerty
retorted that the reports in the *New
York Herald Tribune* didn't even
remotely resemble what he had said
at the briefing. But President
Eisenhower thought the column was
very funny and advised Hagerty to
simmer down.

Art had the last word. The day after
the celebrated column appeared, he
wrote another, taking note of Hagerty's
objections. In this column Art admitted
that he "has been known to write
adulterated rot, but never unadulterated rot."

This man is one of those exceptional
people who never graduated from high

school, but attended college and landed in a career that seems to have been made for him. He was going to high school in Queens, New York, but when he turned seventeen in 1942, he ran away to join the U. S. Marines. He entered as a private and was discharged as a sergeant, and spent most of the time editing his outfit's newspaper on Eniwetok. When he got out of the service he went to the University of Southern California at Los Angeles under the G. I. Bill and became managing editor of the campus humor magazine, conducted a column for the college newspaper, and wrote a variety show. But he didn't graduate from college, either. Instead, he gave in to the desire to try Paris, and it became his beat for a progression of columns about the "lighter things that take place in Europe."

His wife, Ann, is also a writer and literary agent. They have three children and live in Washington, D.C. His office is only a block away from the White House, and it's there, in the shadow of that impressive building, that he writes his political satire.

Washington has become a jogging city in the last few years, and though jogging may not be everyone's favorite form of physical fitness, visitors to Washington can at least get the impression that Washington is for physical fitness. Along the Potomac trails, Rock Creek Parkway, crossing the Memorial Bridge, all the way out to Mount Vernon, and even around the more open areas of the city itself, you can always see joggers.

Once in awhile you'll even spot a celebrity jogger like Senator William Proxmire of Wisconsin, who jogs five miles back and forth to work each day. He runs through the streets of Washington, that include twenty or thirty stoplights, and has narrowly missed being hit by wagons, limousines, and trucks.

Art Buchwald is not a jogger, though. He feels that some people are very uptight and need to do "calisthenics and all those things to feel good," but he doesn't. He thinks exercise is a bore and that it's much better to become involved in a competitive sport of some kind like tennis, which he does.

He does admit getting good walking exercise when he's in New York City. "New York is a great walking city. When I'm there I walk for miles without knowing it. Washington is not a walking city." I would agree with him about that. Washington, D. C., with its lower skyline and more widely spaced buildings, has a feeling of open distances—much better for running than walking. Midtown Manhattan is tightly contained, has many visual distractions, and one really can walk there for long distances without realizing it.

Art says, "A competitive sport like tennis is very satisfying. And it's sure cheaper than skiing or golf. All you have to do is buy a racket and some balls. There are more and more public courts being made available, and a lot of the schools let people use their courts now."

Art Buchwald is an avid tennis player and plays about three or four times a week during the good weather—weekends in bad seasons. It keeps him healthy and in good shape, but even so, he lives with the fact that he is always about fifteen pounds overweight, an aggravation so many people have in varying amounts. He asked me how he could lose it, but realizing he probably already was aware of weight-adding foods and not wishing, therefore, to insult his intelligence, all I could suggest was that maybe he should learn to fret and worry a bit and burn extra poundage off that way. (He happens to be a very unfretful, non-worrying type of person.)

I asked Art to describe his body type to me. "I'd say I'm the Robert Redford type, wouldn't you?"

He is 5'9" and weighs 180 pounds. I'd say he's very lucky he's such an avid tennis player because otherwise a man like him, who has been quoted as saying "I think exercise is dangerous; people should stay in the horizontal position as much as possible," would find himself permanently horizontal in a short time in a coffin built specially for very fat people.

Look at the picture of Art playing tennis. Then study the illustration of the movement that probably followed as

he hit the ball he received, and do it yourself every day in your own home, at least eight times. It might begin to suit you so well that you'll want to play a little tennis yourself after you get conditioned.

I'm a great believer in "mimed exercise," especially for physical sports preparation, because I think it's a very good way to get a feel for the movement style and decide if you like it. Even though you don't know what you're doing technically, your body will know if it's something you want to pursue.

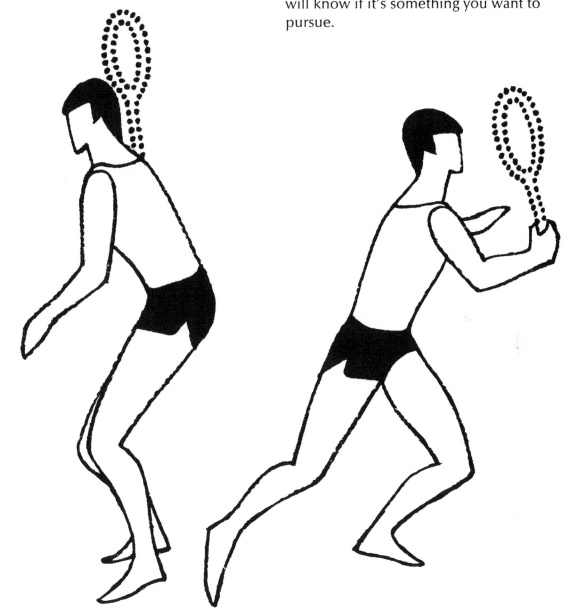

# Totie Fields

☼ *The funny lady of show biz*

THE FIRST television show I ever did was the Mike Douglas Show. The co-hostess of the week was Totie Fields, the comedienne. I never had a chance to feel any stage fright because she kept me laughing, for which I was grateful, and I was able to be quite relaxed and at ease.

After I demonstrated the stretching exercises of the dancer and was interviewed by Mike Douglas, Totie suddenly appeared in leotard and tights for her "exercise lesson," and, of course, the whole audience broke up with laughter. Not only is she round, but the visual contrast on the show of her standing next to me was very funny, because I am quite tall and thin; she stood only a foot above my waist.

It is very difficult to know when to believe Totie and when not to believe her. She will answer a question either with an immediate joke or with a serious comment that turns into something funny. In her comedic conversations we are led to believe that she is a hopeless food addict who's tried every diet and all exercises without success.

Yet, Totie is a very successful comedienne and is not physically hopeless at all! When I began to show her how to exercise I discovered that her body is quite firm and flexible.

She has the short type of body that is always prone to overweight regardless of how closely the diet is controlled—the same type of body that looks enormous when it is pregnant.

Frequently on a talk show someone urges Totie to get up from her chair and walk forward. Then the audience can laugh at the sight of her upper body remaining on the same level walking as it did sitting.

Her ability to laugh at herself and her ability to make people laugh create instant fans. "I didn't start out to be funny," she claims. "It just worked out that way."

She has been performing since she

was ten years old. "I was so intent on becoming a star," she says now, "I used to practice signing autographs."

Her professional career began at the age of fourteen as a band singer while attending Weaver High School in Hartford, Connecticut, where she grew up. At an engagement at the Frolics Club in Boston she met George Johnston who was the comic on the bill and they fell in love, married and had two daughters. It's good to see that their happy marriage has lasted!

Totie had thirty appearances on the Ed Sullivan Show, fifty on the Mike Douglas Show, and guest-starred on almost every television variety show. Her nightclub engagements are always packed, and now she and her family have made their home in the nightclub mecca—Las Vegas.

Totie can be loud and tough on the exterior, but inside she's a real softie. The day I was on the Mike Douglas Show with her, the Everly Brothers were also appearing. The producer of the show had secretly brought in the boys' parents for a reunion. When the reunion took place, Totie, viewing it, was so overcome by the scene that she dissolved in tears.

Another time on the Mike Douglas Show, Arlene Dahl had been discussing her beauty secrets and Totie walked out to the predominantly female audience and asked, "Why do you women listen to her? The odds are you'll never look like her. Better you should listen to me, because the chances are you *will* look like me!"

It was a very funy line, but there *are* many, many women who are built just like Totie Fields and probably would have been interested in her beauty suggestions.

She is a great and much admired entertainer with a strong following. People like her the way she is.

I have never been a large, overweight person, but I have never approved of the "jolly fat" treatment heavy women are subject to, and I've got to believe they don't either. I've watched many television variety talk shows (including the Mike Douglas Show) where fat volunteers are taken from the audience, dressed in sweat suits, and then made to do an exercise segment with the exercise guest, making great fun out of the whole scene. One famous exercise salon motivates women to exercise by telling them they look like baby elephants, and then they exercise to a little ditty that chants "I'm a baby elephant."

Making women figure-conscious and coaxing them to exercise in such negative ways is not at all constructive. But it is done with such consistency throughout our media that it is impossible for many women with an overweight problem to think of their bodies with any sense of pride at all. You can see that general lack of physical pride as women walk down the street or shop in the supermarket— eyes downcast, shoulders slumped, rib cage slipped toward the hips, and total body sag. No amount of diet or exercise is ever going to help, unless a woman first develops, or regains her pride in her own body—whether it's the commercially perfect body or not.

A media exception to the fat/guilt syndrome was a fantastic article done a few years ago by a feminist magazine called "Fat Is Beautiful." It was a fashion spread using the heavy woman, and she was beautiful.

The next time you see Totie Fields on television notice that she has physical pride, and see how much difference it makes. Her shape is secondary.

Totie is constantly "on" and her enormous energy works in her behalf in controlling and burning off more weight than she realizes, for she is not a sluggish person. If she was quiet and passive she would probably be an extremely large woman, unless, of course, she exercised regularly and dieted.

The exercise I taught her on the M Douglas Show is the first one pictur below. Another exercise that would be good for her body type is also illustrated. The diagram shows how this is done.

To do the first exercise, reach the left arm overhead toward the right f slowly, stretching with a gentle bou as close to the foot as possible. Do t four times to each side very slowly, with maximum stretch.

This exercise controls the accumu tion of extra fat on the sides of the

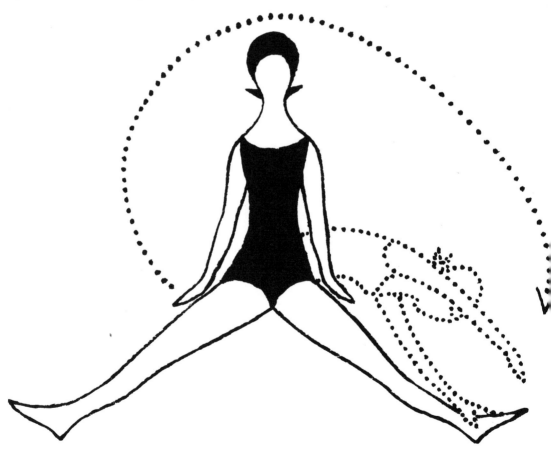

torso and even a part of the thighs and the upper arms. It is an excellent exercise to do without strain to the body. It is especially good for people who are inclined to be overweight, because it helps to maintain a more pleasantly balanced heavy body type.

Totie did the exercise perfectly, and I said, "Your body is not nearly as bad as you say it is."

And she whispered in my ear, "That's because I've been doing this same exercise for years.

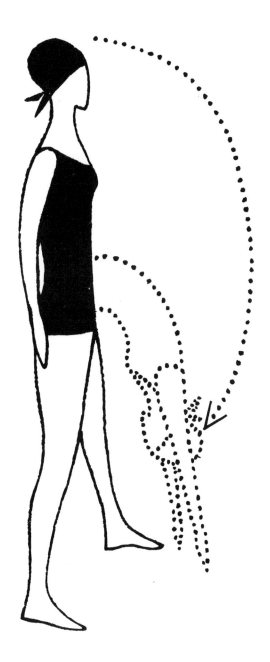

# SPREADING TENDENCIES

Every spreading tendency can be curbed and every spreading problem corrected when you understand the cause. The solution usually begins with a simple reposturing of body position, followed by exercise that reaches and pulls away from the problem area.

Most people don't analyze exercise enough to see what it actually does or doesn't do for their bodies. Much of the spot exercising that people do to correct a spreading waistline, hips, or buttocks actually makes it worse inadvertently by overdeveloping and accentuating the area. The many side-to-side hip-rolling exercises prescribed for reducing these areas actually spread them by breaking down the tissue, just as sitting for long periods of time does.

Every time you pick up a fashion magazine you'll see an exercise to do for spreading waistline, hips, or buttocks. And almost every exercise that is supposed to minimize those areas actually overdevelops them rather than using the muscles around them to pull away from and minimize them.

And almost every time you watch the television exercise expert of the day you can find similar malpractice. I especially recall watching one man say to his woman viewers, "Let me be the engineer and put you back on the track now," as he did a nothing exercise of stepping up on a chair and stepping down again. "Good for the knees and hips," he said, but actually only good for keeping the knee and hip muscles active and reassuring yourself that you can step up on a chair and step down again.

If people would have a little more self-confidence, they'd not let themselves be so blindly led and would assert some initiative in determining and filling their own body needs. Celebrities tend to listen, read, synthesize, and act on their own conclusions much more than the media-influenced public.

One of the reasons a particular area of the body spreads is because it is not used. When you consider our physical evolution, in combination with the fact that as we age our bodies tend to sag downward, you can easily see why the most vulnerable spreading areas are in the lower part of the body.

In our physical and mental evolution we generally use only the upper part of our bodies. We have lost much of our sensory ability and the controlled use of the physical powers that animals use. In losing this type of sensory ability the mind has bypassed instinct and devised extraneous forms of exercise that don't always move the right sets of muscles.

Observe animals, who do not have the highly developed brain of humans and therefore remain sensory creatures, and you will see how instinct integrates exercise into their daily lives. Animals stretch at waking and after periods of inactivity; they react to their body needs and maintain adequate levels of strength for their physical requirements. Every movement the animal instinctively makes favors the development and maintenance of the basic muscles he needs for daily life. Every body position favors the use of the muscles in the lower lumbar, pelvic, and thigh areas—the ones that we let atrophy and then find spreading.

Our hips and thighs must move and support the heaviest loads of our total body weight. We should be able to move from this base of power as animals do naturally, carrying our body weight from an invisible center line of support. This invisible line passes through the centers of the three main bulks of weight—head, chest, and pelvis.

Our bodies can get out of position and become vulnerable to spot spreading because of the roles we play. We must exercise to put them back into shape, and thus strengthen them. As Sylvia Porter said, "My way of life—sitting at a typewriter and bending over a desk for most of the day—would thicken my middle even if I was on a rigid diet."

The female body is constructed in such a way that the waistline is indented. When the upper body slips downward the only place for it to go is the waistline; eventually the waistline indentation disappears so you have to train your body to maintain an uplifted carriage and then exercise the torso musculature so that it can maintain that posture.

You can use any traditional torso exercise, but first inhale and lift your rib cage, creating an extra inch of height through your waist. Then do the exercise—noticing how much more flexibility you feel—and when you finish, continue to maintain that stretch of the waistline. If you don't know any exercises to use, try the ones Sylvia Porter and Arlene Dahl recommend. But first lift up and realign your posture for both standing and sitting positions. You'll find half the battle is won.

# Sylvia Porter

☼ *The widely read financial columnist*

SYLVIA PORTER, the financial columnist read daily by millions in over 350 newspapers, graduated magna cum laude from Hunter College when she was only nineteen years old. In her early days as a financial reporter with the *New York Post* she had to use the byline S. F. Porter because her editors assumed nobody would take a woman financial writer seriously. The times have changed considerably. Her recent book, *Sylvia Porter's Money Book,* has been widely acclaimed.

In New York she walks thirty-five blocks to or from her office each day. "I prowl New York's streets every week," she told me. "When I have a lunch date fifteen or twenty blocks away from my office, I'll walk to and from the restaurant—the same for the theater after work. In other words, if there's a choice between a taxi or walking, and time permits, I walk. And

the more I walk the better I feel." At her country estate in Pound Ridge, New York, she hikes, swims, and pla golf with her husband, Sumner Coll promotion director for the Hearst newspaper chain.

About the first week of January ea year she goes to Arden's famous health spa, Maine Chance, near Phoenix, Arizona, where she exercis swims, and concentrates solely on health and rest for seven to ten days This is a luxury not everyone can afford, yet an example that everyone can apply to themselves in their own lives in their own homes one week out of each year—a concentration o health and rest.

As Sylvia explains, her way of life– sitting at a typewriter and bending o a desk for most of the day—would thicken her middle even if she were a rigid diet. So, every morning throu out the year after coffee and newspaper, she exercises to a fourteen-minute record—"The Happy Puppy" by Bent Fabric—concentrating on exercises for the waistline and abdomen.

She uses the Elizabeth Arden exercises, developed by Marjorie Craig and available to everyone through Miss Craig's book, *21-Day Shape-up Program*. One waistline exercise is called a sitting bend. You sit on the floor with legs spread; clasp hands overhead, palms toward ceiling. Keep legs relaxed, reach to right foot, return to original position, pulling up the rib cage. Repeat to left side and continue. Repeat four times on each side.

Here's an excellent dancer's exercise to follow that you can start from the same position. With hands resting lightly on ankles, stretch, or bounce gently forward eight times, striving to get your head as close to the floor as possible. Return to a sitting position with rib cage held high. Repeat eight times.

The combination of the two exercises is good because of the total movement progression; the first exercise works the waistline area and stretches out the torso with side action, and the second exercise does the same thing to the front.

The most important thing to remember is to lift the rib cage as high as possible before doing the exercises so that you cause a waistline separation between the upper and lower body. Keep your chest high throughout.

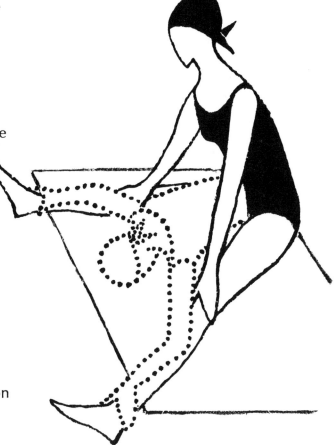

# Arlene Dahl

☼ *Star of stage, screen, and television*

ARLENE DAHL'S name is synonymous with beauty. Apart from her acting career—twenty-nine films, twelve stage productions, and a television series—she has written fourteen books and numerous syndicated beauty columns. In private life she is the wife of Rounseville W. Schaum (Skip), Chairman of the Board and Chief Executive Officer of International Telecommunications, Inc. She was born in Minneapolis, Minnesota, of Norwegian descent, and exemplifies that glowing, healthy Nordic look.

She has a very pretty face; her skin is especially beautiful. She could probably get through life with a terrible figure and no one would ever notice. The figure she has is the Lillian Russell type—38-25-37.

"I was one of those late bloomers and until seventeen or eighteen didn't even *have* a figure," she told me. "The top half of me was a size eight and the bottom half a size ten. Having children improved this and really put my figure in proportion. Now both halves are size ten." (She has three children.)

Arlene's general body maintenance is copied from her cat "P.J." who never makes a move from a lying-down position without first stretching one extremity at a time, slowly and carefully. Each morning as Arlene wakens she reaches for the headboard with her hands (stretching one arm at a time) and the end of her bed with her toes (stretching one leg at a time.)

This gets the motor running. Then she stands up and reaches for the ceiling, first one arm then the other, then both. From the waist she bends over and bounces forward like a rag doll, touching her toes. Her feet are six inches apart for this.

She winds up her morning routine with a windmill exercise, which serves to check any possible waistline expansion and also helps to smooth and tighten the hips, the spreading area that she must contend with.

To do the windmill exercise, stand with feet apart; raise arms above the head, and in a sweeping motion twist from the waist, touch the toes to the right, around to the left, and back up to your original position, arms still above the head.

Repeat twice to the right and reverse. Move from the waist only; the body from the waist down should face forward throughout. Do not let the body return to a sagging position when you finish. Keep the good posture of the sweeping stretch.

A few years ago Arlene conceived the idea of her Beautysuit, which she designed to wear for exercising. During her appearance on Broadway in *Applause* she tested it for total use, wearing it during her dance routines, rehearsals, and on stage under a flowing caftan. "It slims and trims, and when worn over a good moisturizing lotion keeps the skin soft as silk," she says.

Special outfits for exercising cause mixed reactions. It is true that the most ideal garment to use for exercise is the dancers' leotard and a pair of tights, the basic idea of Arlene's design. It is akin to a second layer of skin and therefore so sensitive that you feel the exercise from the inside and see your exterior movement clearly, thus making it easier to correct flaws. The ideal garment for exercise clings comfortably to the body and moves with it.

But the psychological effect of donning a special outfit for the purpose of exercise acts as a deterrent for many people who will then skip the idea because it's too much trouble. My suggestion has always been to put on a leotard and pair of tights (or a

garment like Arlene's) first thing in the morning on a day when you will be at home. Wear a shift or pair of pants over it so that you are dressed for a normal day but can quite easily peel off for an exercise session.

Arlene walks a lot, breathing deeply as she does because it helps keep her skin glowing. For general posture, body tone, circulation, and figure streamlining, Arlene thinks the stretching exercises are excellent.

A Lillian Russell type of figure is a lovely figure to have if kept in well-balanced proportions. "I have hips," Arlene said, "which of course are great for childbearing but not so great for wearing straight skirts or slacks. So I have to work on my hips daily."

Her special hip exercise is a body roll from side to side done with knees bent and lying on her back. The higher the knees are held the greater the benefit to the hips, because the greater is the tightening pull on the back stretch line from the waist to thighs.

If you suffer from spreading hips I would suggest you double Arlene's recipe by repeating the morning windmill exercise right after this one, so that the hips get a total workout each day. The beneficial emphasis on the body roll is really across the buttocks, even though you think you are "rolling down" the sides of the hips (it's the buttocks tightening that's allowing the sides of the hips to be drawn in—not the rolling on them). The windmill exercise pulls up and off the extra bulk on the sides of the hips.

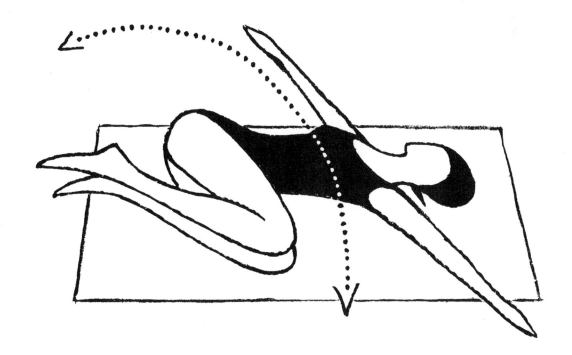

CRAIG PHOTOGRAPHY

# Frankie Welch

☼ *Scarf designer for the famous*

DANCERS have their leotards and tights for exercise; Arlene Dahl has her Beautysuit that she designed and wears; Frankie Welch recommends an all-purpose apron that can be worn over such exercise outfits as camouflage.

Frankie Welch is a designer who achieved fame with her scarf designs. For Lady Bird Johnson she designed the "Discover America" scarf; for Hubert Humphrey in 1968 she came up with the HHH scarf; then there was the famous Cherokee Alphabet scarf, and more than seven hundred others. When the Fords went to China a few years ago, Mrs. Ford took a selection of Frankie Welch scarves to present as gifts.

Mrs. Gerald Ford is one of the many famous customers who has found her way to Frankie's tourist attraction boutique in Old Town, Alexandria, Virginia. It's also an attraction for the many political women in Washington who find her clothes to their liking.

For professional reasons, as well as personal, Frankie must keep a good figure. She's a devotee of the stretch exercises, because they proportion the figure best. "I think they also help control your posture; you can't be beautiful in clothes without good posture," she said in her soft, Georgia-bred voice.

In her home she has exercise pictures taped to places like the refrigerator as reminders not to eat too much and to exercise every chance she gets. "I have to be on guard all the time, lest my waistline spreads too much."

After explaining to her how she must learn to keep the rib cage separated from the hip area, she reciprocated by giving me the apron pattern she designed, which is reproduced here.

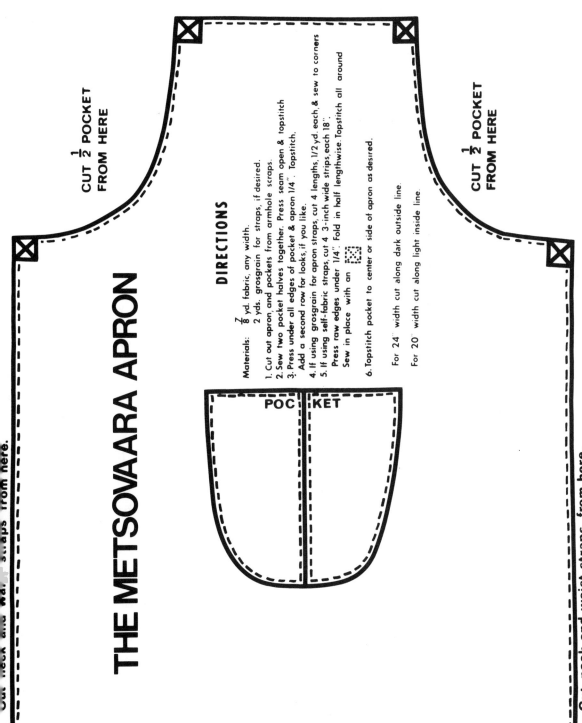

# THE METSOVAARA APRON

CUT $\frac{1}{2}$ POCKET FROM HERE

CUT $\frac{1}{2}$ POCKET FROM HERE

POCKET

## DIRECTIONS

Materials: $\frac{7}{8}$ yd. fabric, any width.
2 yds. grosgrain for straps, if desired.

1. Cut out apron, and pockets from armhole scraps.
2. Sew two pocket halves together. Press seam open & topstitch together.
3. Press under all edges of pocket & apron 1/4". Topstitch. Add a second row for looks, if you like.
4. If using grosgrain for apron straps, cut 4 lengths, 1/2 yd. each, & sew to corners
5. If using self-fabric straps, cut 4 3-inch wide strips, each 18". Press raw edges under 1/4". Fold in half lengthwise. Topstitch all around Sew in place with an
6. Topstitch pocket to center or side of apron as desired.

For 24" width cut along dark outside line.

For 20" width cut along light inside line.

Cut neck and waist straps from here.

Cut neck and waist straps from here.

# Marian McPartland

☼ *A smooth, sophisticated jazz pianist*

"**I** STILL have the dress I opened in at the Hickory House in New York City in 1952, and it fits me just like it did then. It's one of those strapless dresses that aren't in style anymore, so I can't wear it, but I do put it on every once in a while just for kicks. If it's a little tight in places I cut down on my eating and try to move around a bit more."

Marian McPartland, the jazz pianist, is 5'6", well-proportioned and healthy. She hates to see people let themselves go, and intends never to let it happen to her. When asked about her specific exercise habits or style, she said she really never thought about exercise as a special function. The only definite answer she could give me was that she walks every place she can because the body needs movement just as it needs food and rest, and walking is the best exercise she knows. I was talking to her about exercise at Michael's Pub in New York City where she was playing; she had walked over from Penn Station, a distance of about 1½ miles. She did this every night during her engagement there, since she commuted from the suburbs.

The last time I had heard Marian play the piano in person was 1957 in Milwaukee, and before that, in Chicago in 1949 with her husband, Jimmy McPartland, jazz cornetist whom she had met and married during the Second World War.

She was British, playing in USO camp shows. She and Jimmy met in St. Vith, Belgium, where she sat in on a jam session in his honor after he returned from combat to join Special Services. After they married, Marian joined Jimmy's band as pianist.

As I listened to her playing boogie-woogie and bebop and improvising on the old standards, the music sounded as great as ever. And I noticed that her body hadn't changed in twenty years. That's quite amazing for any woman or man, because the shape of the body is bound to reflect twenty years of living.

"It's probably because I'm very perceptive about my body," Marian explained. "I'm careful about what I eat—neither overindulging nor following fad diets. I'm eating less meat—not because I don't like it any more, but because I mind the brutal killing of animals. I can control my well-being simply by heeding the signals my body sends me. When I feel some inertia or general body slowdown coming on, I know I need an extra workout."

An extra workout means going out to rake the leaves or working in the garden. She doesn't like making exercise separate from her regular routine; it's time consuming to go someplace special to do exercise when you can make it a natural part of your daily life. She walks. She runs. She does a lot of things around the house. And now that she has her own record company (Halcyon Records) she always seems to be stretching up high to get records off a shelf or moving boxes from one place to another. Occupational movements integrated into a normal day can round out exercise needs quite well, as long as they're not done tensely, under strain.

"There are all kinds of things you can find to do if you really want to. I play tennis once in a while because I love the game, and now I'm thinking of taking up squash again, because I like it even better—and it's so fast."

Marian has a great store of energy, and in addition to her performing dates in the evening, she likes to work in the daytime doing short sessions in the public schools, playing for the children, and getting them to play. She loves this as much as they do.

Halcyon recently released "Solo Concert at Haverford College," and before that "While We're Young—Marian McPartland Plays the Music of Alec Wilder." Marian is one of the great performers of the jazz piano. She is known for her delicate touch, subtle harmonies, and impeccable technique.

Her musical training in England was traditional, but she fell in love with jazz after hearing Duke Ellington, Count Basie, Art Tatum, and Teddy Wilson. When she was offered a chance to tour with a four-piano act, broadcasting for the B.B.C. and recording for Decca, she accepted it, went on the road, and made jazz her life. She ranks with Mary Lou Williams as one of the greats.

Some of the compositions she's written are: "A Delicate Balance," "Melancholy Mood," "Solace," "Illusion," "Ambiance," "Lost One," "Aspen," and "Afterglow." Sarah Vaughan and Johnny Smith recorded her "There'll Be Other Times"; Tony Bennett recorded her "Twilight World." She was in attendance at the White House a few years ago for Duke Ellington's seventieth birthday celebration. Recently I heard her play at Blues Alley in Washington, D.C., and she sounded better than ever.

Even though Marian is a naturalist

when it comes to exercise, she's got the best recipe of all to control spreading tendencies in the hips and buttocks. It's the very reason why she, a woman who sits at the piano for hours, does not have an enlarged "seat" or the "secretary sit," as I call it.

Call it what you wish, it amounts to one thing—hips and buttocks that grow too large—and it is generally accepted as the occupational hazard of the woman who sits all day on the job. It's always been the major complaint of the office worker who sees herself spreading over the years and feels helpless about doing anything to stop it. But it's unnecessary and it is avoidable. It's the result of improper weight placement in the sitting position.

Marian McPartland sits just as long at the piano each day—and even into the night—as any secretary, but her "seat" stays properly proportioned to the rest of her body because years ago she discovered the correct weight placement. You can't see the entire sitting position in this picture, but you can at least see the angle, which is completely different from many of her male piano-playing contemporaries. Many of them have, incidentally, become enlarged over the years in that very spot. Being male or female has nothing to do with it; it's where the weight is placed.

The secret is in the precise way you sit. It's the same way a dancer is trained to sit, with the weight evenly distributed throughout the body so that movement, or action, is possible instantaneously in any direction. If the largest concentration of body weight is in one place, the rest of the body is immobilized in that position in a totally sluggish way.

Lift your body weight out of the hips, up through the torso; lean very slightly forward so that the weight is more properly distributed throughout the uplifted torso and supported by the bones and muscles at the end of your spine rather than the fat on the underside of the buttocks. Make any slight adjustments in your position until you feel secure and in control.

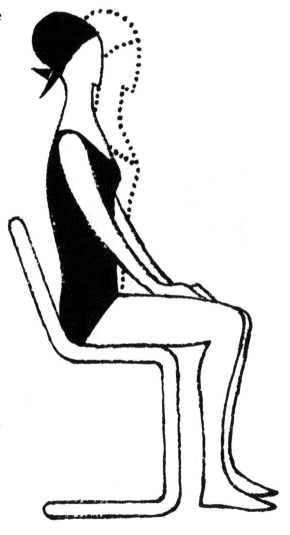

When you sit for long hours on fat it flattens out and spreads. When you sit as Marian sits, you keep that from happening and you also feel more energetic because you're able to maintain a lightness of feeling in place of the heaviness that results from misplaced weight.

Even if you sit with a perfectly straight back in a right-angle sitting position, you are sitting with too much of your body weight resting in your hip area—and there it will stay and accumulate over the years. But, if you lift and shift your weight with a slight forward incline you can redistribute that weight and prevent the spreading.

By the way, you don't have to be a secretary or a jazz pianist to be able to use this exercise. It's for anyone who cares about the size of his or her posterior.

# PROBLEM AREAS

PROBLEM AREAS is a catchall heading to cover the miscellaneous figure irregularities that aren't included in sections on age, weight, bone size, spreading, bad backs, and arthritis.

The ones represented and dealt with quite successfully by the celebrities here are humped shoulders, loss of stomach muscle tone resulting from childbirth, large hip/thigh structure, protruding stomach, and leg length.

Not represented are things like fat accumulations along the sides of the ribs, flabby arms, cellulite, under- and overdeveloped legs.

Fat that accumulates along the sides of the ribs is very easy to work off. To begin with, hold your body high at all times to prevent the extra fat that forms when you let your shoulders drop. Then choose any stretching-type exercises that pull away from the fat accumulations. Any movement that pulls away from an area of fat, with the whole body involved, will minimize that area, redistribute and work off the extra fat. The stretching exercises work most successfully because of the way they extend the muscles rather than

tightening and enlarging them within the contained body. Any stretching movement that employs the same motion you use for reaching up high for something will help.

Many spot exercises prescribed for specific areas only make them worse, because they tend to use those same muscles over and over again, isolating the muscle action from the rest of the body; lots of action but no improvement. Even though a particular exercise may be done for a specific purpose, it can't accomplish that purpose unless it is working with the cooperation of the entire body.

There is an exercise in this chapter which I recommended to Joan Rivers for minimizing heavy hips and thighs. This same exercise (sit on floor with legs spread and reach for toes) is also excellent for working off rib fat, if you do it the way I told Joan to do it: by turning the palm upward there's a line of body stretch that extends the entire length of the side of your body. When you do a side-stretching exercise, which activates one entire side, you shift and work off any excess that happens to be along that line.

You never see a dancer with fat accumulations anyplace in her body. That's because she is always exercising along her natural stretch lines, and her body stays proportionate that way.

As women age, their upper arms become flabby and unattractive, either because they never used the muscles in these areas enough or because they stopped using them at some point in their lives. Movements that flex these upper arm muscles will help retard flabbiness. It's been said that Mae West lifted weights to keep her bosom high. If that is true I suspect that it also took care of any upper arm flab. (Interest in weight-lifting among women has increased with the women's movement because of the desire of many women to develop their bodies and have stronger muscles.)

It's a good idea for every woman to take advantage of every opportunity she can to flex and use her upper arm muscles. To correct upper arms that are already sagging badly, do some isometric exercises (pushing or pulling against an immovable object such as a wall). If you've never done isometrics before, start easily. Don't apply your maximum effort in the beginning. Do little breathing during isometric muscle contractions, but breathe deeply between them.

Every once in a while someone comes up with a word to label a particular body problem. Cellulite is one that has become familiar lately. It's a word to describe the dimpled fat that some women acquire. The hip/thigh area is the most vulnerable spot

for this kind of fat. The cure is about the same as the other fat-reducing methods—eat less fat-producing foods (especially greasy foods), exercise, and correct the diet. But you'll have even greater success if you realign and correct your posture so that the vulnerable cellulite areas don't exist for you. Stretching exercises will help to smooth them out.

If your calves are overdeveloped you must learn to counterflex them. Any exercise you do in which you can feel the pull up the backs of your legs will help minimize those heavy calves. One good exercise for this is to bend over with straight legs and touch the floor in front of you. And notice the way you go up the stairs; if you're only using the front half of your foot you should change that habit and make sure you place the whole foot on each step so that your calves don't flex with each step.

Of course, if your legs are skinny and underdeveloped, you'll want to walk up stairs on the front half of your foot only, forcing the calves to flex and build up.

Jogging may be very good for body circulation, but it is inclined to build up the calf muscles. If they're already large, I suggest you temper your jogging with some other form of exercise. On the other hand, if you have skinny legs you might want to start jogging!

A figure problem can usually be solved quite simply if you can determine the cause. Think about the cause and then do something logical about it.

# Pauline Trigère

☼ *Award-winning fashion designer*

Award and the NBC-TV Today Show Fashion Award as "most original designer,"among others. On June 22, 1972, at the Hotel de Ville in Paris, she received the Silver Medal of the City of Paris.

There was solid fashion design preparation for all this from her childhood. The daughter of a dressmaker and a tailor, Pauline was born in the heart of Paris, Place Pigalle. She had no special training, but learned to cut and fit in her father's tailoring shop, and when quite young made her first *toiles* (muslins) at the then celebrated house of Martial and Armand, Place Vendôme.

Her brother Robert, who helped guide her budding taste and set the standards of her craft, was her business partner from 1942 until he moved recently to California. Now her two sons are in the business—one as comptroller of Trigère Inc. and the other as head of the Trigère perfume division.

For several decades she has kept her place at the top of the changing fashion industry. This can be attributed to her talent for producing deceptively

IN 1942 Pauline Trigère set up her own business in New York with a collection of eleven styles. Since then she has won every major American fashion award; she is a three-time winner of the Coty Fashion Award, and in 1959 received the fashion world's highest honor, the Coty Hall of Fame Award. She has won the Neiman-Marcus simple clothes with intricate and bias cut. In the classic tradition of Vionnet, Lanvin, and Chanel, Trigère does not sketch; she cuts and drapes directly from the fabric, and in so doing has pioneered an extraordinary number of fashion themes—innovations that eventually turn up in the Seventh Avenue lines.

Pauline is 5'4½" and claims to be a size twelve, but she looks much smaller and taller. Everything she does includes exercise. "I am not a static person, and I am forever on the go; I'm working and moving my body unconsciously most of the time. I go on foot wherever possible. I run up the steps. Even when I am on the telephone I exercise; I might put my leg high on a wall or on the edge of a table and stretch my body to keep a constant flexibility; or I might put my hand on the table nearby and push my body away from it slowly to keep my upper arms firm.

"And one exercise leads to another; the trick is to learn to let your body discover and do all the exercises that help and are good for you. It would be difficult to name a favorite exercise. There are different exercises for different body problems; and we feel different each day, depending on moods or what's going on in our lives.

"Exercise is very important to me, and I seek extra movements in addition to my normal daily routine. I am capable of exercising by myself, but I have a Yoga teacher who comes to my apartment two or three times a week in the early morning (I only sleep five hours a night) to check my 'form' and my breathing, but mostly to keep me working instead of answering the phone.

"As you grow older, you know, everything about your body goes down, a little like a soufflé, so you must exercise and stretch, stretch, stretch in all directions. If, for some reason, I am not able to exercise for two or three days, I start slowly when I resume. And I don't do anything that would strain the heart; that is why I like Yoga so much—you do what you can, no more, without competing."

"Generally I keep my weight stable. I am inclined to pick up a little extra when I prepare a collection (I eat and drink constantly). But then I know how to stop and keep the weight in check. If I feel too big in the waist, I force the waist exercises.

"If I didn't watch it, I think the busy schedules and the worries of the business would make me hunchbacked. To stop stooped shoulders, I believe in reverse exercises to adjust and counterbalance what your body does all day."

What Pauline specifically means is that you must be aware of the way your occupation and your daily habits alter your basic posture line. Then you can exercise to counteract any incorrect positions that would become set permanently over a period of time.

Pauline is very perceptive about exercise, and in stating her vulnerability to stooped shoulders is well aware of the hours she spends hunched in the concentrated positions of cutting, draping, and fitting that pull her shoulders forward. How easy it would be for her body to become set in those positions if she didn't counterbalance them with appropriate exercise.

You can frequently guess a person's profession by watching his or her body. The actor will be poised with the uplift of body projection; the humble servant's body withdraws; the construction worker is muscularly developed for his job; the draftsman, the tailor, the garment worker become stooped because their shoulders are hunched over while performing the concentrated movements of their daily work.

A body often becomes distorted and misshapen as a result of the occupational posture which it assumes day after day, and year after year. Fatigue and tension result, for when you adapt your body so that it is strained and out of alignment, extra energy is expended.

If it's an occupation that uses small movements of the eyes and hands, and requires many small decisions and judgments and constant attention—sitting at a desk, typewriter, or microscope, for example—you become tense, because your subconscious mind/body must be constantly ready to restrict any major movements. Fatigue comes from tension.

If that same fatigue is combined with worry, anxiety, or pressure, the distorted body position and its movement becomes more rigid. And body position also influences the emotions, so there is a constant physical/emotional process going on that stylizes and sets you in strained position. Pauline Trigère keeps this from happening to her because she is aware of the danger.

There are many exercises one can do to offset the distorted postures that result from certain professions. The Yoga stretches and positions are especially good, and the one that immediately comes to mind that Pauline uses is the Yoga Cobra (or snake).

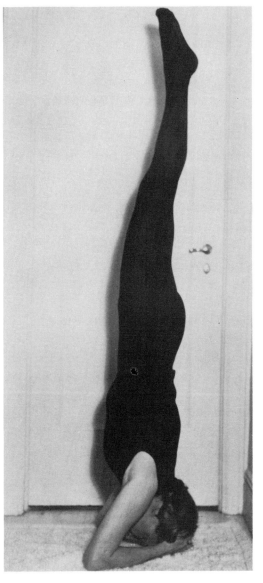

Lie on your stomach. Put your hands on the floor at shoulder height. Slowly push up your upper torso by pressing on the palms of your hands and stretching the arms as far as they will go. The torso becomes arched and the head stretches back as far as possible. The feet are stretched out at the end of the legs and the lower part of the body —from waist to feet—remains on the ground.

Inhale deeply through the nose as you get off the floor. Stay in the position as long as you can with your arms stiff and your head back, holding your breath the entire time. Bend your arms, and return to position, exhaling slowly.

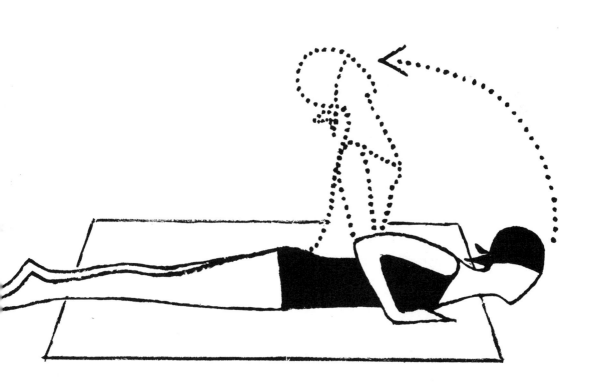

*STANLEY TRETICK*

# Eleanor McGovern

☼ *South Dakota's famous author and lecturer*

"A STRONG family should be the birthright of every child. If we could think child and child care, then no longer would our children be hurt first and most by every flaw in our society. It is a myth that people instinctively are good parents; much good parenting has to be learned. I advocate parenting classes in junior and senior high schools and college. We go into the most important responsibility of our lives being quite ignorant of the needs of children."

Since her husband's presidental campaign in 1972, Eleanor McGovern has been traveling about the country trying to make people aware of their responsibilities toward our young children.

In her book, *Uphill, A Personal Story,* which she wrote with Mary Finch Hoyt, Eleanor talks about growing up on a South Dakota farm during the Depression, and of the great hurt she suffered as a little girl when her mother died. She believes her grief could have been absorbed much better if her family and the community had let her share it with them rather than isolating and insulating her from it.

In her life as the wife of a presidential candidate who attracted great numbers of idealistically committed youth, she saw similar needs that prompted her to study the whole subject of child development and determine specifically just how important parents and communities are to the formation of a child's future happiness and place in society.

She generally talks about the needs of emotional development, but is equally cognizant of the physical aspects of growth and its relationship to the emotional.

"I think very few people can function well mentally, physically, or emotionally without a good exercise regimen. Our bodies were meant to be used. I don't mean that we should go overboard on the subject of exercise and let it become an obsessive thing; is should be a natural part of our daily lives, and with the proper balance of exercise, nutrition, and peace of mind, we are free to do our best in our chosen area of endeavor."

She herself exercises twice a day, ten to fifteen minutes each time—partly calisthenics and partly Yoga stretching. She walks as much as she can; in stores she goes up stairs instead of using elevators. She parks her car some distance from her destination, which necessitates more walking. When she feels morose and gets the blues, she rides a bicycle out in the country. This always lifts her spirits.

"I've found how easily exercise can fit into one's day. Many tell me that they know it's good for them but they can't stick with it because it's boring. I think the Yoga keeps it from becoming boring. It is absolutely fascinating to see what the body can do. It stretches and becomes more flexible in just a short time. I can stretch at least three inches in a few minutes. Exercises that I think I'll never be able to do—for instance the Yoga Plough—I find I can do after a few days. This flexibility of the body and the continued evidence of it is a constant source of amazement. There is also a feeling of well-being and a noticeable relaxation that follows —much more relaxing than taking a nap."

Eleanor McGovern is small and slender, and after five children had to work at firming the abdominal muscles. For this she does calisthenic sit-ups and sit-backs, forcing a tighter muscle tone in the entire abdominal area.

It's difficult to exercise right after childbirth because of the fatigue that accompanies the new home routine. When you finally do get around to exercising, so much time has passed that you must work doubly hard to get the muscle tone back. If you force yourself to exercise under chaotic conditions, you can do more harm than good because you're inclined to exercise too tensely, and force your body out of alignment.

Because I was raised in dance, it was easier for me to get back into shape after giving birth. I automatically did isometric improvisation (tightening/

releasing action of the stomach muscles in standing, sitting, and reclining positions). This is what the doctors should really stress after pregnancy because it can restore the muscle tone to a satisfactory "holding position" until things around home settle down.

The Yoga Plough that Eleanor does is also very good for tightening the stomach muscles. I recommend you do the Yoga Plough after the sit-ups and sit-backs, because as you go into the Plough position you unconsciously pull the stomach muscles in toward the spine and hold them there during the entire time you hold the Plough position. No amount of "pulling the stomach in" in a standing position can do as much.

To get into the Plough position push yourself up to the Yoga Candle position, which is the starting point, with toes pointed toward the ceiling. Keep your legs straight and bring them over your head toward the floor behind you. As Eleanor said, eventually you will be able to touch.

The purpose of this exercise is to be able to get into this position. Once this is achieved, stay as long as you wish.

Eleanor also has two favorite exercises that tone up the stomach muscles, and involve total body movements. First stand with feet slightly apart, arms stretched overhead and behind ears with fingertips touching. Inhale and stretch forward as far as possible with arms behind ears and fingers touching. Exhale and return to position. Turn from the waist to each side and repeat. She does this about fifteen times each morning. This keeps the rib cage high, out of the waistline area, so that the stomach muscles can be "reached" and pulled up tightly by the action of the arms.

Later in the day, when she finds the time, she sits on the floor with soles of feet together and does this exercise: Grab toes with hands and pull them upward to bending head. Hold briefly. Repeat four times.

To get even greater and more correct benefit from this exercise, alter Eleanor's style and do it like the ballet or modern dancer does, grabbing your ankles instead of toes (when you hang on to toes you twist ankles, and ankles don't like to be twisted). Pull your head gently, as close to the feet as possible. This pulls the stomach muscles in taut and also works off any extra fat accumulation on the backside.

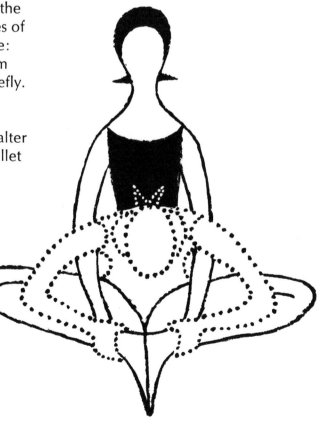

# Joan Rivers

☼ *The outrageous comedienne of TV and nightclubs*

"I REALLY am an unexercisey kind of person," Joan Rivers told me. "I tend to be heavy from the waist down, and the only exercise I do consciously to try to keep my thighs nice and firm is to swim."

Swimming is one of the best figure-shaping forms of exercise there is. It pulls excess weight out of the hips because of the forward pull of the body against the force of the water. The thigh muscles become tightened with the leg-kicking action that is coordinated with the swimming strokes.

Comedienne Joan Rivers graduated Phi Beta Kappa from Barnard College at nineteen and reached her present status as a performer by working up through the Borscht Belt and a variety of clubs. She helped work up sketches for "Candid Camera" and wrote comedy material for Phyllis Diller and Zsa Zsa Gabor before appearing on the Johnny Carson Show and going on to wider fame. She's married to producer Edgar Rosenberg and has a daughter.

Being a comedienne has nothing to do with body type, and Joan's figure is nothing like Totie Fields's, but you might find it interesting to know I recommended the same exercise for both of them. It's the exercise I prescribe most often for the greatest variety of figure problems.

For Totie's body this particular exercise controls the extra fat accumulations on the sides of her torso. But for Joan and people who are only heavy from the waist down, the exercise is done for a different reason —to reduce the size of the hip/thigh area. The magic of the exercise is that it does what the body needs.

I think this exercise is one of the most effective "figure shifters" there is. Along the natural line of stretch that runs up the sides of the body from kneecap to elbow you can have a proportionate shifting of misproportioned bulk and work off extra inches.

I first discovered the use of this exercise many years ago when I worked with models who were trying to shape themselves to specific proportions. This was the exercise we could count on—if done regularly— to achieve the most well-proportioned body possible for each individual frame.

For general proportioning, you do it the regular way, (the Totie Fields way). In sitting position spread your legs and then very slowly reach to the side of your foot. Repeat exercise twice on each side.

For moving extra inches out of hips and thighs (the Joan Rivers way) turn your palm upward as you do the exercise. This forces a stronger pull out of the heavy area. Pull on your ankle to the count of ten; return to upright position and reverse sides. It has such an effective pull that you will actually feel like the side of your torso is going to tear. If you do this exercise regularly you will first notice a reduction in hip size; when the extra bulk is worked out of the hips the exercise then begins to pull bulk out of the thighs and minimize them the same way.

HERBERT EISENBERG

# Selby Kelly

☼ *Pogo's cartoonist*

THE first time I ever noticed Walt Kelly was in 1936 at the Walt Disney Studios where we both worked. I was working in the building across from him doing inking and painting, which was all a female artist was allowed to do at that time regardless of how well she could draw. I never actually met him though until 1968 at MGM. Shortly after that we were married.

"I'd always been a fan of his. As a matter of fact, a group of us would get together and have a party and act out the latest Pogo comics, each of us taking the part of one of the characters, and reading aloud."

Walt Kelly is dead now, but Pogo, the plucky Okefenokee swamp hero that he created in 1949, will live on in the comic strip collections of America.

Selby kept the Pogo strip going until the newspapers, in their cutback of pages, reduced the size of the comic strips so much that people complained that they couldn't even read the lettering. Selby thought it wise not to subject Pogo to such indignity.

Pogo probably had a few wise things to say about exercise; Selby does, too. "I'm inclined to be too heavy, but my exercises work so well I don't keep them up, and only use them when the situation gets out of hand. I think you can learn to control any body problem if you apply a little common sense.

"For instance, I have a bad back, but I've learned how to keep it from bothering me. The trick is to maintain good posture. If you keep your torso

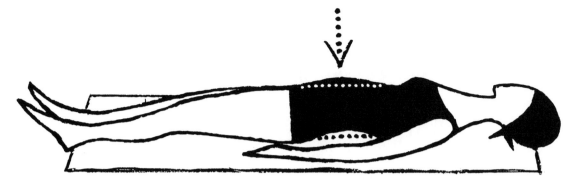

straight and balanced (cantilever style) you can lift and do all kinds of things without strain."

Selby is 5'4" and weighs 140 pounds, plus or minus, depending on how much she lets it fluctuate before considering herself too heavy. "My biggest problem is my stomach, so I have to correct that frequently."

Her corrective exercise is good, and it involves using the muscles that usually become weakened by a large stomach. Selby does it often enough to have control; for those of you with large stomachs who are not used to the exercise and cannot feel the muscles you must use, here's a simple preparation.

Lie on your back; tighten the stomach/buttocks muscles area in such an exaggerated way that your knees rise slightly; hold and release. Repeat this tightening/releasing action six times, so that you are aware of your specific muscle strength, which is what you will be using in a standing position.

Stand in good posture and pull the stomach in slowly to the spine to a count of six; hold briefly, and relax. Repeat six times. Make sure you are actually pulling the stomach in with its own muscle control and not with a massive inhaling action. Do this each day until you regain the muscle tone necessary to control your stomach.

It's a good movement to practice frequently. It doesn't drastically reduce the size of your stomach (food quantity is the factor there), but it does help you keep it in line.

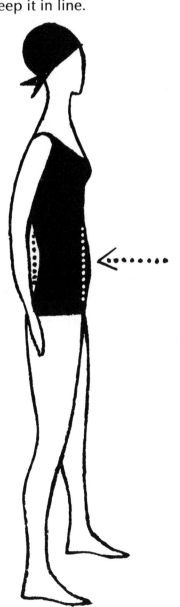

# Polly Bergen

☼ *Movie star and vital businesswoman*

WHEN Polly Bergen was eleven she weighed 145 pounds, had reached her full height of 5'5", had a forty-inch bustline, a forty-inch hipline, and a twenty-five-inch waist. "A terrific figure if you're twenty-five; if you're eleven, it can really get in the way," she said. "I was the only girl to flunk physical education three years in a row because I wouldn't get undressed and take a shower with the rest of my classmates. They thought I was dirty, but I was the only person in class with breasts, and I was horribly embarrassed." *At fourteen, though, her body and sophistication were an advantage; she looked much older than she really was and was singing professionally.

Recalling Polly Bergen in various films and looking at her today, it's har to imagine her figure as less than perfect, but she openly admits that sh is badly proportioned. She no longer has the 40-25-40 figure of her youth; she does have a very long torso, an indefinite waistline, and short legs. Al her leading men, including Gregory Peck, who's about 6'3", had to have pillows placed under them when they were filmed sitting down.

She's clever about it, though, and disguises these structural body problems with careful attention to the clothes she wears. By concealing her waistline she can make it look higher than it actually is and create the illusion of having longer legs; wearing high heels makes her legs appear four or five inches longer. Poise and good carriage also draw attention away from her misproportions, which would otherwise be quite obvious.

She cannot physically change her long torso and short legs, but by regular exercise she can keep everything else about her body in perfect shape so that her basic figure faults are diminished. Early in her movie career she started working with Marvin Hart, the masseur and exercise authority who works with many of the Hollywood greats to keep them in shape. Polly says since that time she has "never had serious worries about her figure. Once you get on to a system of exercise that works for you, you never forget it and return to the exercises quite easily.

When her hips were too large she used the following spot-reducing exercise: Stand with legs apart and grasp the elbow of your right arm from behind your head. Moving from the waist, bend as far as possible to the left so that you are actually pulling the fat out of the hips. Hold for a few seconds and straighten slowly. Do this ten times on each side.

It is a misconception to think that you reduce a large body area by exercising that area by itself. What actually happens is that you accentuate and overdevelop it. The most effective way to minimize a large area is by doing exercise that pulls away from it as Polly did with her hip exercise.

Polly likes to use a slantboard for some of her exercising. A slantboard costs about twenty-five dollars or more.

For those who think they, too, would like to use a slantboard but don't want to spend the money she suggests making one yourself by padding a bench. Or be creative and look around your home for something you can use as a facsimile if you really want to work on a slantboard as she does.

The exercise pictured below is done for general torso tightening and control. It also strengthens the upper body, which results in better carriage. When you develop a good, strong, proud carriage in your upper body you take on a poise that is complimentary to your body no matter what type it is. Notice that performers walk with a slight uplift to their chin, which elevates the entire upper body and adds to their poise. If they dropped that physical control they would become indistinguishable from everyone else. You can do this same exercise without a slantboard by lying flat on the floor on the rug and anchoring your toes under the couch or heavy piece of furniture. Using the furniture does eliminate the need for a special place to use the slantboard.

To do it as shown in the picture, sit high on the slantboard and anchor your feet under the straps; fold hands over your chest, and then lean backward slowly, as far as possible; straighten up to a sitting position. Do the exercise in three sets of ten—thirty times in all—resting after each ten.

Polly Bergen says that any woman who spends more than ten or twelve hours a week on her appearance is close to falling into a beauty trap. She believes that exercise is more important

to good looks than all the makeup and hair preparations put together (even though she is president of her own cosmetics company), because it keeps the body vital through good circulation.

Even when she is traveling, Polly manages to do about fifteen or twenty minutes of exercise every morning, and if commitments interfere in the morning she exercises in the evening. If she doesn't exercise every day she's tired, regardless of how much sleep she gets, and doesn't even enjoy her food as much. When she feels fatigued she exercises for a pickup. Exercising to combat fatigue is energizing. Try substituting an exercise break for a coffee break sometime and see how much better you feel. You'll find you can get much more work done and feel less fatigued, too.

Polly is the head of the Polly Bergen Company, a cosmetics company which is a subsidiary of Fabergé. A few years ago she made the Oil of the Turtle famous as a moisturizer for the mature woman with extra-dry skin. (Oil of the Turtle was a by-product of the turtle meat industry; turtles weren't killed for the sake of producing cosmetics.)

Her latest addition to skin-care products is called Original Skin, a collection of cleanser, rinser, day moisturizer and night moisturizer made from a base of natural grapeseed oil. Original Skin is a collection programmed to help protect the skin of the woman between the ages of seventeen and thirty-four. Natural grapeseed oil is supposed to be highly effective because it glides on easily, is extremely light to the touch and on the skin, and is absorbed readily.

Before she became a cosmetics company business executive, Polly Bergen had a very successful performing career covering about thirty years on stage, screen, and television. She is probably best remembered for her award-winning performance in *The Helen Morgan Story*. She was born July 14, 1930, in Maryville, Tennessee. She sang and danced by the age of two, and was singing professionally at fourteen. She has been married twice and has three children. She's one of those women who look absolutely perfect at any age, and probably always will, because she takes such good care of her body.

# Alessandra Greco

☼ *A dazzling dancer in the Spanish tradition*

"MY FATHER says I'm like a Chihuahua but built like a Great Dane, and all my dance teachers said I should never become a dancer because my hips and thighs are too big."

Father is the famous Spanish dancer, José Greco, and the names of the dance teachers who discouraged Alessandra are not important, for the fact is, she's dancing with her father's company, is very involved with drama, and fully expects dance to be a part of her future in the theater.

I can understand a dance teacher warning a young girl about the odds against being accepted as a professional dancer if her body is drastically incongruous with the visual demands of the craft, but I have known many dancers and performers who have risen above such supposed handicaps and turned them to advantage. Determination and drive can bring a basic talent to very exciting fruition.

The artistic lineage for this girl is very strong; she is a blend of her parents, bearing the characteristics of both the dance style of her mother and her father. Her mother was one of the seven Natya Dancers (Hindu Dance) of La Meri in the forties when she met, married, and became one of José Greco's Spanish dancers. Alessandra's father, José Greco, had partnered the great Spanish dancer Argentinita until her death, and was in the company of her sister, Pilar Lopez, before forming his own company in 1948.

Alessandra went to the High School of Performing Arts in New York City, joined the José Greco company as a replacement on tour when she was twelve years old, and has been dancing with the group ever since. She's twenty now—a spirited, poised girl who is 5'7" and weighs 135 pounds.

She is a stately young woman who cares about her body. Even at twenty, she has learned what to do about weight control and body problems in order to have the physical perfection that she desires and is so important for her as a performer.

Her solution to body problems is in the exercise of the dance. The development of her strong, poised, proud, uplifted carriage, is so evident and impressive that the size of the hip/thigh area is subordinated to it. The style of the Spanish dance itself—that proud peacock bearing that is so beautifully exciting—is a part of it.

The exercise Alessandra likes best, which helps to create this illusion, is a simple, uplifting, even happy exercise. Sit on the floor with torso held straight and proud, legs spread, toes pointed, arms open to the sides, parallel to legs. Bring your right arm in to body center front as knee pulls up to a count of one, raise arm high over head to the second count, and lift head. As arm breaks open at the height of the lift the whole body opens up, and the arm returns to the beginning position to counts three, four. Alternate arms and vary count for different body accents, but always be aware of the uplift. Repeat eight times on each side. The exercise is refreshing, and helps to establish the high carriage that is so attractive.

# ARTHRITIS AND BAD BACKS

A GIRAFFE has seven vertebrae in its neck, the same amount people have, but you never hear of the giraffe having as many vertebrae problems as people do. Those seven cervical vertebrae of ours compose the neck and hold up the head.

Holding up the head is the point I've been trying to make throughout this book, saying it differently in each section so that you can eventually understand that the most important thing you can do for your body physically and emotionally is to hold up your head. When you do, you pull up your whole body and make it easier to maintain proper alignment; you also move with the poise of a person with pride, and body pride flatters any figure, regardless of size or shape.

Now I must mention another aspect of holding up the head, which has to do with back problems. Eight million people are being treated for back trouble these days, and much of it begins with neck-spinal misalignment, which can do severe damage if not corrected—and frequently already has by the time signals of pain are received.

When you have back pain, you don't feel like holding up your head!

Many back strains come from occupational postures combined with worry and tension, which create a muscular imbalance. Conscious efforts to relax these muscles will stave off future back problems of a more serious nature. One way to relax the back when you are standing is to imagine a line drawn down your back and up your front. This imaginary line will keep your bones at proper levels for a balance of body weights.

Some back problems are the result of laziness and generally poor posture. The only way to overcome laziness is to get into something interesting and stimulating; both body and mind benefit from that.

The easiest back problems to solve are those that come from structural misuse, because understanding body structure allows you to make the mental adjustments that correct this problem.

For instance, women who wear high heels over a long period of time eventually experience a forward tilt to the pelvis, accentuating the curve of the lower back and creating lower back pain. It's a good idea to vary heel size so that you don't get into these patterns, even going barefooted whenever possible.

If you allow your stomach to protrude, there is constant tension in the small of the back. Relaxing the back muscles and correcting your posture allows the spine to straighten and draw in the abdominals. When you lie on your back in bed, be conscious of the feeling in your body, not just its mirror image. This will help you to let go; with the bed under every segment of the body your skeletal muscles can rest properly.

The longer a person's back, the greater the weight to be carried. In a body that has a long back, the lower vertebrae are large and the ligaments and muscles joining them will be strong and tight, limiting the movement in order to secure strength. As I mentioned in the chapter on large bones, such backs are vulnerable to strain because they are not designed for extreme flexibility. If one tries to force movement, pressure is created on the discs in the lower back.

But the body needs flexibility to prevent muscle strains in general. Many muscular problems, which may be diagnosed as rheumatism or arthritis, are simply the result of severely limited flexibility. If calcium deposits form in the joints because they have not been used sufficiently, the result is an arthritic condition that may be hard to cure.

Rheumatism used to be the general name of many diseases that affected the muscles, ligaments, and tendons of the body. If a person found it impossible to lift her arms above her head or bend her leg to any extent, she might suffer the pain, call it rheumatism, and resign herself to old age. But the fact is that such cases of "rheumatism" could be caused by muscles that haven't been stretched properly.

Arthritis is a group of ailments involving joints, muscles, and tendons. The common types are: infectious arthritis, a form which accompanies diseases such as tuberculosis and rheumatic fever; metabolic arthritis, characterized by excessive quantities of uric acid in the blood (gout); osteoarthritis, a chronic disease of the joints in which there is degeneration of bone and cartilege, usually just seen in older people; rheumatoid arthritis, which affects young as well as old, and in advanced stages results in joints becoming immovable. Women tend to be more prone to rheumatoid arthritis than men, and men more susceptible to metabolic arthritis (gout) than women.

Both Lady Bird Johnson and Betty Ford have a touch of it. If you do, too, maybe you'll get a little help from this section.

# Lady Bird Johnson

☼ *Former First Lady and America's beautification champion*

THE image projected by Lady Bird Johnson is that of a happy, healthy, vibrant person. And that she is. She is also a lady—a woman who has learned to maintain a gracious, pleasant appearance and manner at all times under all circumstances, regardless of how she feels.

That's not always easy, for everyone knows distress, trial, and tribulation, in some form at one time or another—even Mrs. Johnson, who admits to a bit of arthritis and has suffered physical reactions to stress and strain, though few would know it.

What's her secret? In her words, "Buoyancy—a general feeling of well-being, which is very important to me."

She creates this buoyancy by being physically and mentally active, and she maintains it by being enthusiastic about life. As all famous people, she has an awareness of self that is necessary for success as a person. Buoyancy becomes her.

She generates her feelings of well-being with morning exercises. "The older I get, the stiffer I get! So I exercise for thirty minutes every morning—the standard bending and stretching exercises that everyone knows—and I find the more I do the better I feel. I know it helps control my arthritis." She even does an occasional bend or stretch between appointments at the LBJ Library in Austin, Texas, where she has an office.

Swimming and walking are part of her physical life, too—especially walking. Mrs. Johnson walks with enthusiasm, and she walks to discover. Many a companion has been worn out trying to keep up with her as she walks about one of her many beautification projects (presently the Town Lake project along the Colorado River in Austin), checking the progress of the plantings or looking for signs of early-blooming Texas wild flowers. Frequently she will break up an "office type" day by going for just such a walk.

Lady Bird Johnson made her mark as First Lady by turning America's attention to the beautification of our surroundings. It was something that benefited the country and aptly served as an expression of herself.

The continued interest Mrs. Johnson has in her various beautification projects and the walking she does to oversee their progress definitely work to her advantage now by providing a continuity of outdoor activity that is health giving—especially in the country where the air is cleaner!

As a businesswoman Mrs. Johnson is involved in the operation of radio station KLBJ, a cable television company in Austin; she is executor of the Johnson estate and actively committed to the LBJ Library and the LBJ School of Public Affairs at the University of Texas, to which she gives freely of her time and financial support. The list of trusteeships, governing and advisory boards she serves is endless. Though we hear of her less frequently since she left the White House, she is far from idle and works just as hard, if not harder, than she did when she was in the limelight.

Lady Bird Johnson feels that the application of a person to ideas, to work, and to achieving goals is vital to successful living and to the enjoyment of life. Her enthusiasm overcomes the minor irritations that tend to slow one up both physically and mentally. By paying attention to the positives and putting one's energy there, the negatives are diminished.

When asked if there was anything about her figure that she considered a negative, she laughed and said, "At sixty-two, I guess I'm stuck with myself the way I am."

But knowing about her arthritis and the therapeutic value of warm-water exercising, I recommended this exercise for her. It's a very soothing movement to be done in the bathtub. Of course it can also be done sitting on the floor, as shown in the illustration, but you do get more out of it in warm water.

With hands holding ankles, slowly, gently, pull the head as close to the knees as possible to a count of four, exhaling; inhale and return to the sitting position and hold briefly. Repeat four times. The warmth of the water as the body stretches slowly is most effective in relieving lower body stiffness, and the pull of the stretch movement up the back line of the body is such that the figure is kept firm and in good shape.

This exercise is also good for pulling a tired back into alignment, stretching out the spine and straightening it as the head goes toward the feet. If you're going to do this exercise or copy it for a friend, make sure you begin correctly

—with your weight pulled upward from the buttocks so that you are "unlocked" in the lower spine and ca go forward with ease. Some people will be able to touch head to knees and some won't, but both receive eq benefit. It's the maximum stretch tha important—not whether you can touch your head to your knees or no

There is equal opportunity to use warm water for therapeutic exercise while taking a shower. Any one of the standing stretch exercises Mrs. Johns does in her morning exercise session can also be done in the shower. The occasional bends or stretches she do between appointments in her office can also be performed in the shower.

A simple one that is quite effective is to reach slowly for the ceiling, one arm at a time, as many times as you

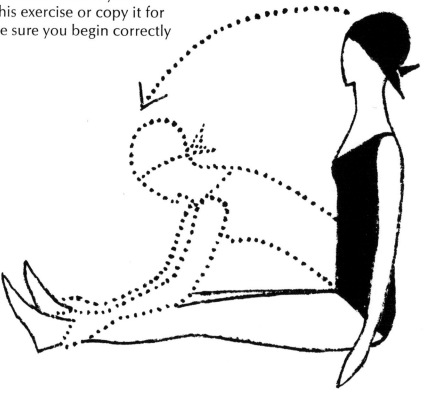

feel comfortable (at least eight times), making sure the warm water is hitting your shoulders and back. The warm water provides extra therapeutic benefit.

This particular stretch movement is also very good for general posture. It coaxes the entire body upward, thus countering its tendency to slip downward with age.

The only restriction in shower exercising is the actual size of the shower. If it's a bathtub shower your movements must be restricted, but if it's a square shower unit you can feel freer to move.

Mrs. Johnson does not make a great "to do" over the fact that she, too, among millions of American women, has arthritis. Because she's a positive, vibrant person she really is less concerned with it than she is with the rest of her life, and you would therefore never know she has discomfort from it occasionally. But she did give me permission to make a point of it for the sake of others who might, through her example, be able to help themselves to more exercise and learn to have a little of the buoyancy that she says is so important to her.

# Sarah Palfrey

☼ *An all-time tennis great*

SARAH PALFREY is the most famous of the Boston Palfrey sisters, each of whom have won one or more national tennis titles. From 1926 to 1969 she won thirty-nine U. S. National Titles and twenty-four Foreign National Titles, and was on ten U.S. Wightman Cup teams.

Sarah is now with *World Tennis* magazine, and plays tennis in the New York area two or three times a week—mostly mixed doubles. She's the wife of Jerry Danzig, a radio/television executive and the mother of two grown children. Her last national win was the National Senior Hard Court Mixed Doubles Tournament in Seattle, Washington, in 1969; Sarah and Alphonso Smith won over Kitty Prince and Len Dworkin—a memorable event because she and Alphonso Smith had last played together forty years before when they won the Massachusetts State Juniors together.

In the thirties Sarah played tennis with Helen Wills, Bill Tilden, Betty Nuthall, Helen Jacobs, and Alice Marble; and in the forties Pauline Betz, Fred Perry, Enrique Maier, Don Budge, and Jack Kramer. She was only fourteen the first time she played at Forest Hills.

Tennis was so important to Sarah that she passed up college and attended art school nearby instead. Her father was the very distinguished lawyer to Oliver Wendell Holmes, but it was her mother who was athletically inclined and responsible for introducing the Palfrey family to tennis and making it possible for them to excel.

In 1941 she won the U.S. Singles National Championship, and in 1942, in her eighth month of pregnancy, was teaching tennis to the Navy wives at Pensacola, where her first husband, Elwood Cooke (also a tennis player), was stationed at the time.

"After the birth of my daughter in 1942 everyone thought I was through, but three years later I won the U.S. Singles again." In 1946 she retired from competitive tournaments and wrote her first book, *Winning Tennis*, turned pro in 1947, and toured with Pauline

Betz. She was elected to the National Tennis Hall of Fame in 1964. The picture below shows her playing at Forest Hills in 1930.

We talked about women and sports in general and I asked about the great Babe Didricksen Zaharias, who excelled at every sport but tennis. Babe never reached her potential in the game of tennis, though she spent a lot of time trying and took lessons with the best teachers, including Eleanor Tennant, Alice Marble's coach. Sarah felt it was probably because she was too aggressive and tried to make a winner out of every shot instead of practicing strategy.

Many people will remember seeing Sarah as both interviewer and guest on the NBC "Today" and "Home" shows. She also was moderator of her own "Girl of the Week" show, and frequently broadcast play-by-play commentary and interviews at tennis

matches across the country. Former Mayor John Lindsay appointed her a Sports Commissioner of New York City.

Even though she gets plenty of exercise playing tennis about three times a week, Sarah has an unvarying procedure she follows for extra exercise twice a day—morning and evening —in the interest of general health and flexibility, but also for the purpose of controlling minor arthritis.

When she awakens in the morning she stretches slowly in all directions. Her stretching involves her whole body and she gives extra attention to wrists, fingers, and toes where the arthritis is inclined to settle. (She also plays the piano every day, for her fingers, emphasizing octaves and tenths.)

Then, while still in bed, she pulls her knees up to her chest, points her feet to the ceiling, and lowers her legs. She does this five times to tighten her stomach muscles.

After she gets out of bed, she continues her stretching routine with twenty bend-downs, touching the floor in front of her. Then she does imaginary tennis serves—forehands and backhands—making a point of alternating arms so she won't become lopsided. In the evening she repeats the whole process in reverse.

It's a simple routine to follow, and her exercise plan is for anyone, just as the title of her most recent book, indicates about tennis: *Tennis for Anyone.* The stretching, the knee to chest movement, and the bend-downs are standard body movement. But an analysis of the movements she does to control her arthritis shows an excellent progression of hand-to-arm exercise that is quite valuable for people who have arthritic tendencies.

The progression begins within the framework of her total body stretching as she gives extra attention to wrists, fingers, and toes. She finishes with the imaginary tennis serves, forehands and backhands, which involve the hands and the larger movement of the arms.

Many women have to live with arthritis. Sarah told me that all the women in her family have a touch of it. She is convinced that the pain is alleviated by exercise. She also makes sure that the vitamins she takes include minerals, which is advice her doctor has given her.

Sarah worked out with me the following hand-arm routine. It's especially good because it begins with the hand stretch in which you extend

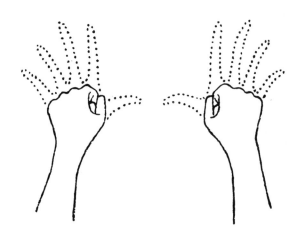

fingers to maximum from a fist position eight times; then with stretched fingers you force a total hand workout by pressing fingertips against fingertips ten times; finish with a gracefully executed hand, arm, shoulder movement (simulated tennis serve) four times on each side. This relates the hand stretching to the rest of the arm and body. Even when you do spot exercising for a specific purpose you should always finish the movement by involving it with the rest of the body.

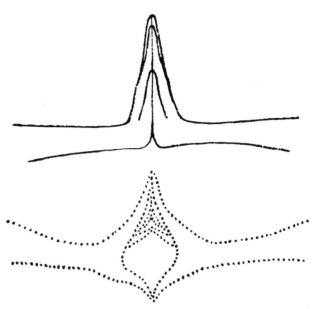

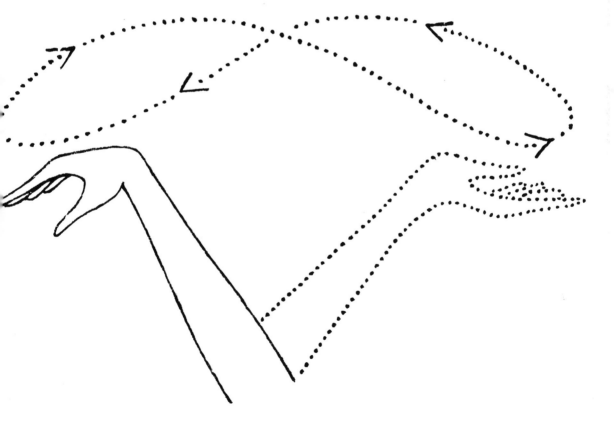

# Rosemary Prinz

☼ *Daytime television's foremost star*

To THE millions of people who have watched the CBS television serial "As the World Turns" over the years, Rosemary Prinz is Penny. She also starred in "All My Children" on ABC, was seen in a ninety-minute special for ABC called "Courtroom One" and the NBC serial, "How to Survive a Marriage."

The theater, however, is her first love. She began at the age of sixteen at the Cragsmoor Summer Theatre directed by Morton Da Costa, and since then has trouped all over the United States in a variety of plays. On Broadway she starred in George Abbot's revival of *Three Men on a Horse*. During the last few seasons she has appeared with David Canary, Tom Poston, Tony Tanner, Art Carney, and Gabe Dell in plays on and off Broadway.

In *The 90-Day Mistress*, the play Rosemary was starring in when I met her, one of her lines was, "Well, you must admit I've kept my shape." This line automatically drew the attention of the audience to her figure, and you could hear a low murmur of approval going through the theater, for Rosemary does have a most attractive shape; she's 5'1" and weighs ninety-six pounds.

That most attractive figure is not without its back problems, however, and when Rosemary is on the road she always finds a good doctor or physical therapist nearby who can give her relief when she needs it. When she is in New York City she goes to the studio of Carola Trier two to four times a week for body conditioning and correction.

The problem stems from muscle tension, which causes bones to get out of alignment and results in much discomfort. Along the spine, from the head down, are muscles that are like two ropes that support it on either side. They tighten and distort as a result of our fatigue and tension; the tension is not something we are aware of until we notice back pain. It is difficult to prevent because it's practically impossible to remain relaxed at all times in our modern-day living. For the actress, or performer of any kind, there is the tension connected with rehearsals, performances, traveling, and other pressing situations.

Carola Trier has many actors, dancers, and performers coming to her for body conditioning and rehabilitation, and many of them owe their "performing lives" to her. She uses the "muscle contrology" of the late Joseph Pilates, plus her own knowledge of anatomy and understanding of the needs of each individual, to help restore and strengthen full body use. Her exercise tables are equipped with springs. Her students use the resistance of the springs to push and pull against in performing their exercises.

She reached this technique after a back injury forced her to discontinue a career in dance and acrobatics. After rehabilitating her own back with the help of Mr. Pilates, she began to specialize in body rehabilitation, conditioning, and correction.

Throughout this book I have repeatedly referred to the need for correct body placement and alignment. When we speak of back problems it takes on even more importance.

At the suggestion of Rosemary Prinz I visited the studio of Carola Trier in New York City, talked to her, learned her technique and watched her help strengthen and correct people's bodies.

Her way of making body placement more graphic is to compare it to a building. If postural relationships are in any way faulty the whole structure may be wobbly and weak, as a building would be if its constructional relationships were out of line. The foundations of the human body are two feet, each of which rests on a tripod of the big toe, the little toe, and the heel. On these foundations rise the legs as twin columns. At the top of these two columns is the bridge of the pelvis. This is comparable to the firm basement foundation from which rises the "upper stories" of the rib cage, shoulders, and head. If you do not stand on your feet correctly you can put your whole house "out of order."

Since Rosemary Prinz and millions of other people have nagging back problems that need frequent exercising, I thought it would be helpful to devote some space to specific back-relaxing exercises that can be done on your own (with your doctor's approval, of course). The exercises are a blend of Carola Trier's movements and my own. They should help your neck and shoulder tension as well as loosen up the back muscles.

From a prone position, lift your he and press it as closely as possible to your chest as you inhale and pull you knees to your chest. Grasp your ankle but keep your elbows out to the side. Then press your chin to your chest, your knees to your chest, your abdomen to your spine, your spine to t floor, and exhale. Return to original position. Repeat four times. Do the same exercise one leg at a time, pulli and guiding each knee as shown in t diagram.

Standing in a good posture with fe

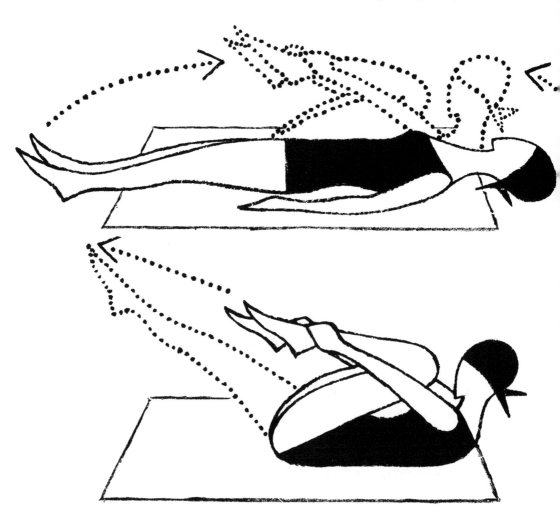

apart, roll your shoulders forward so that your back is "opened" and your chest tucked under. Bend your knees, press your abdomen to your spine, and "open your back" further. Then roll up from the base of your spine, straightening your knees as you come up. Make your shoulders come all the way up before letting them fall naturally into place. You can do the same movement in a kneeling position. Repeat four times in each position.

JOHN TITCHEN

"**A**RTHUR MURRAY Taught Me Dancing in a Hurry" was the novelty song by Johnny Mercer that Betty Hutton sang in the movie *The Fleet's In* way back in the forties. The Arthur Murray Dance Studios are still teaching people to dance throughout the

# Kathryn and Arthur Murray

☼ *America's legendary dance team*

United States, even though Kathryn and Arthur Murray have been retired in Waikiki Beach, Hawaii, for about ten years.

Arthur Murray became an American institution in the forties by teaching ballroom dancing and establishing studios in every major city in the United States. In the fifties and sixties he and Kathryn were seen frequently on television dancing together on her show and as guests on other shows. They still dance together, and I'm sure this has played a vital part in their continuing good health. They also play tennis together two or three times a week.

Arthur's favorite exercise is swimming; he likes the backstroke because the arm and chest motions offer him the most muscular exercise. One of the extra benefits of swimming that should be mentioned is the fact that the pressure of the water on the body promotes deeper lung usage.

"The only exercise I use is for strengthening my back muscles," Kathryn said. "Many years ago I had a spinal fusion, and when my back gives a twinge I immediately go to my short, twice-a-day session. I was originally told to do each exercise only five times a day. Since I am in fairly good muscular condition, I start by doing each ten times, twice a day, and gradually work up to twenty times, twice a day."

These are the exercises, given to Kathryn by a physical therapist, which should be done at least four times.

1 *Pelvic Tilt:* Lie flat on the floor, or an exercise pad, or thick carpet. With knees bent, arms at the sides, pull the stomach in as you tighten the buttocks and flatten the back to the floor. Relax before repeating. Then do same exercise but with legs straight on floor. In standing position with back against the wall and feet about four inches from the wall, do a pelvic tilt so that waist is pressed against the wall. Relax before repeating. Then stand away from the wall, and repeat pelvic tilt.

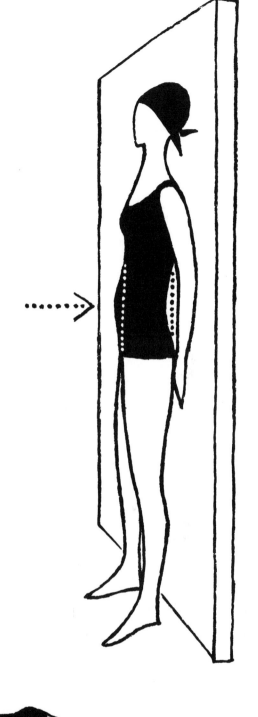

2 *Alternate Knee to Chest:* Lie on floo
with both knees bent and maintain
the pelvic tilt as you raise one knee
as close as possible to chest. Repeat
with the other knee. Then repeat
with both knees together. Relax.
Then repeat.

3 *Partial Sit-ups:* Lie on floor, knees
bent, feet flat on floor and arms at
sides; raise head, then shoulders,
curling upward toward knees.

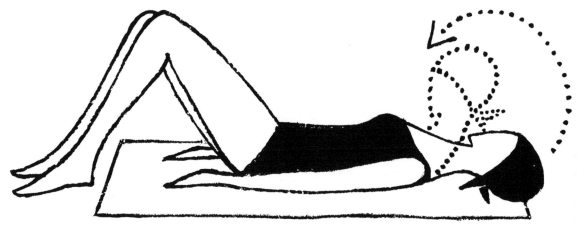

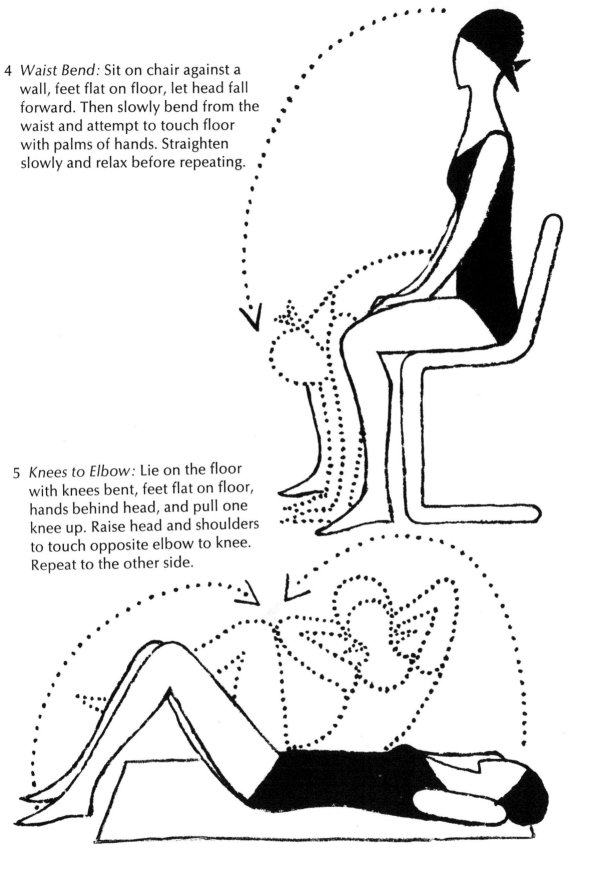

4 *Waist Bend:* Sit on chair against a wall, feet flat on floor, let head fall forward. Then slowly bend from the waist and attempt to touch floor with palms of hands. Straighten slowly and relax before repeating.

5 *Knees to Elbow:* Lie on the floor with knees bent, feet flat on floor, hands behind head, and pull one knee up. Raise head and shoulders to touch opposite elbow to knee. Repeat to the other side.

**KATHRYN AND ARTHUR MURRAY** ☼ 159

# AFTERWORD

ONE OF the most rewarding aspects of individual freedom is the pleasure that comes from making your own choices. When you consider all sides of a subject and draw your own conclusions, it is personally satisfying. I have great respect for the individuality of people and their ability to make choices when given the opportunity.

Therefore, what you've read, take from it what you like, and add some ideas of your own. You will be pleased with the results because you will have "exercised" your individual freedom.

—*Ann Smith*